BHS

AQA BUSINESS
for

SETTING UP A BUSINESS

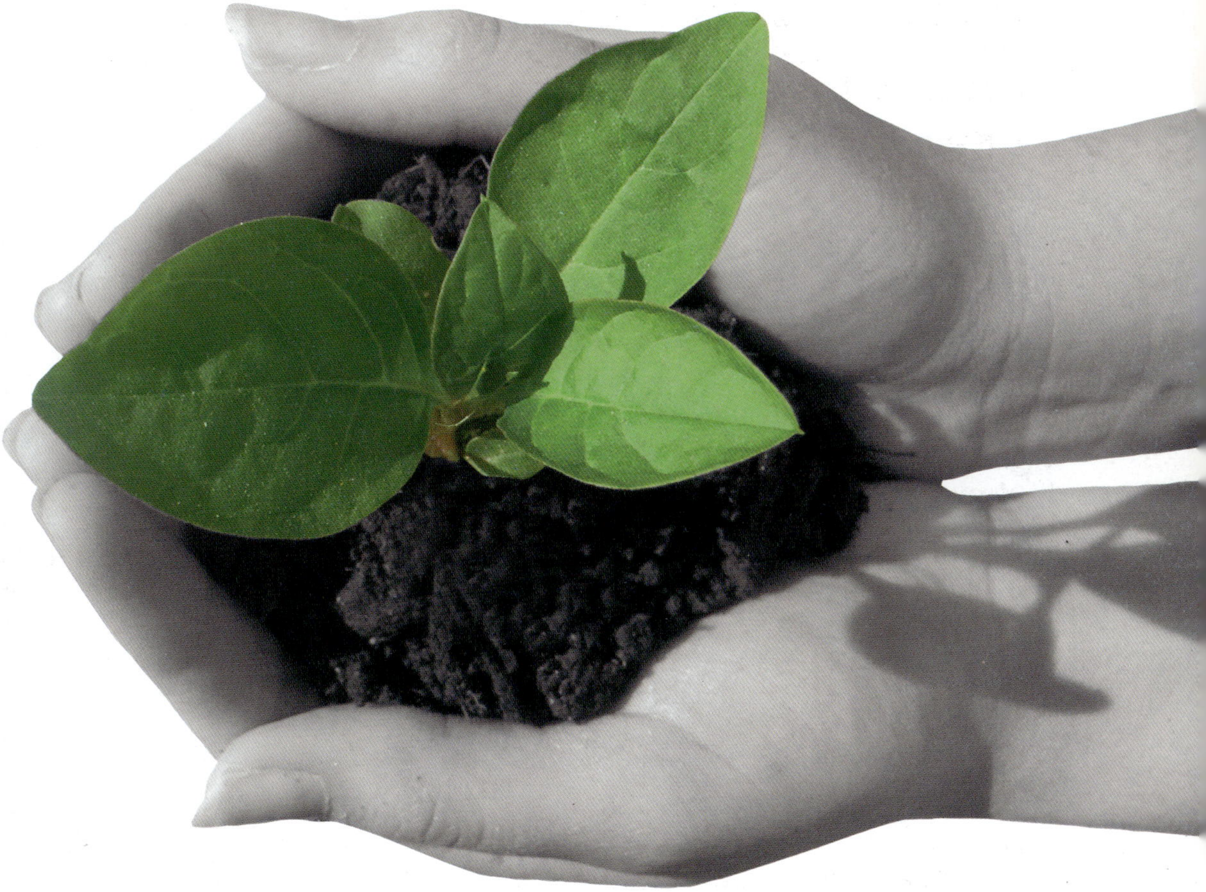

NEIL DENBY

DAVID HAMMAN

HODDER EDUCATION

Orders: please contact Bookpoint Ltd, 130 Milton Park, Abingdon, Oxon OX14 4SB. Telephone: (44) 01235 827720. Fax: (44) 01235 400454. Lines are open 9.00–5.00, Monday to Saturday, with a 24-hour message answering service. You can also order through our website www.hoddereducation.co.uk.

British Library Cataloguing in Publication Data

A catalogue record for this title is available from the British Library

ISBN: 978 0340 97492 6

First Published 2009

Impression number 10 9 8 7 6 5 4 3 2 1

Year   2015 2014 2013 2012 2011 2010 2009

Copyright © 2009 Neil Denby and David Hamman

All rights reserved. No part of this publication may be reproduced or transmitted in any form or by any means, electronic or mechanical, including photocopy, recording, or any information storage and retrieval system, without permission in writing from the publisher or under licence from the Copyright Licensing Agency Limited. Further details of such licences (for reprographic reproduction) may be obtained from the Copyright Licensing Agency Limited, Saffron House, 6–10 Kirby Street, London EC1N 8TS.

Hachette UK's policy is to use papers that are natural, renewable and recyclable products and made from wood grown in sustainable forests. The logging and manufacturing processes are expected to conform to the environmental regulations of the country of origin.

Cover photo © iStockphoto.

Typeset by Phoenix Photosetting, Chatham, Kent.

Illustrations by Oxford Designers and Illustrators.

Printed in Italy for Hodder Education, part of Hachette UK, 338 Euston Road, London NW1 3BH

Contents

The AQA GCSE Business specification   v
How to use this book   vi
Acknowledgements   ix

SECTION 1

Defining Business and Enterprise   1

Chapter 1	What is business?	2
Chapter 2	The nature of markets	8
Chapter 3	Taking risks – enterprise	14
Chapter 4	Reducing the risks of starting a business: Franchising	20
Chapter 5	Business aims and objectives	26

SECTION 2

Starting a Business   33

Chapter 6	Stakeholders	34
Chapter 7	Planning an enterprise	40
Chapter 8	Types of business structure – unlimited liability	45
Chapter 9	Limited liability companies	50
Chapter 10	Business location decisions	55

SECTION 3

Marketing   61

Chapter 11	Researching the market	62
Chapter 12	Marketing mix elements and price	68
Chapter 13	Marketing mix elements and product	73
Chapter 14	Marketing mix elements and promotion	79
Chapter 15	Marketing mix elements and place	85

SECTION 4

Finance   91

Chapter 16	Sources of finance	92
Chapter 17	Business support	98
Chapter 18	Keeping accounts	104
Chapter 19	Making a profit	110
Chapter 20	Managing cash flow	116

SECTION 5

People in businesses   123

Chapter 21   Recruiting staff   124
Chapter 22   Rewarding staff   129
Chapter 23   Motivating employees   134
Chapter 24   Staff and the law   139
Chapter 25   Other legal responsibilities of business   144

SECTION 6

Operations management   149

Chapter 26   Producing a good   150
Chapter 27   Providing a service   155
Chapter 28   Small businesses and ICT   160
Chapter 29   The importance of customer service   165
Chapter 30   Protecting the consumer   169

Preparing for the Controlled Assessment   174
Index   177

The AQA GCSE Business specification

The AQA GCSE Business specification is based on the 'story' of a small business enterprise which can then successfully expand. Unit 1 is called 'Setting Up a Business' and looks at the business concepts and ideas that are needed to establish a small business – and at how that business might measure its success. Unit 2 shows how the business could grow, and the changes that it would have to make along the way as it developed. Unit 3, Investigating Small Businesses, follows this through by asking you to apply your knowledge to a business that you are asked to study. Many businesses do not grow beyond their small beginnings so, if you are taking the short course, you will only study Setting up a Business and Investigating Small Businesses.

This book covers the Unit 1 part of the specification:

- It covers how the idea for a business might be created, how a gap in the market could be found (or made) and how an entrepreneur might go about filling that gap.

- It looks at the reasons why people want to go into business – not always just to make money, but for independence, or to carry out an ambition.

- You will study how a business sets its targets, how it plans and locates, and the way in which it must handle its legal paperwork.

- Of course, a business is unlikely to sell anything unless it lets people know what it is selling, where, when and at what price. You will therefore study the nature of markets and how a business markets its products.

- It is important to know how a small business raises and records its finance, and the tools that it can use to help it to manage its accounts.

- In addition, you will look at how a business recruits its people, makes them want to work hard and keeps the best of them.

- How are the operations of the business carried out? This is the final section in Unit 1.

Unit 2 shows how the business could grow, and the changes that it would have to make along the way. It might need a different legal structure, for example, or its growth might cause problems among its stakeholders. As it grows, it is likely to change its targets: personal success or independence may no longer be enough; the business might want to become the biggest in its market, or even to expand overseas. Much will change as the business grows – the marketing mix will be different, larger businesses are financed differently and, with larger and more complex organisational structures, might need to be organised more formally.

Finally, in Unit 3, you will use all that you have learned to investigate a real business and present those investigations in a professional – businesslike – manner.

The specification is designed to encourage you, through your study, to think about the practical aspects of business and how the concepts and ideas that you learn can be applied in the real world. It also provides a good route to higher qualifications such as AS and A level and the Advanced Diploma in Business, Administration and Finance.

How to use this book

This book provides information, exercises and materials to cover the learning required for the first part of the new AQA GCSE Business Studies Full and Short courses.

The new qualification has several routes, but all begin with 'Setting Up a Business'. This unit is an introduction to setting up and running a business, and looks at the factors that might help the business to succeed, or cause it to fail. It also shows that businesses operate within societies and communities, and that they must therefore take a number of people and their views into account when operating.

From this starting point, you may go on to take one of the following routes.

- Take the **Full GCSE** by studying how businesses grow and completing a coursework-style assignment called a Controlled Assessment. The Controlled Assessment is explained on page 175 of this book. The unit on business growth is covered in a companion book, *AQA Business for GCSE: Growing as a Business*.
- Take the **Short Course GCSE** by completing a coursework-style assignment called a Controlled Assessment. The Controlled Assessment is explained on page 175 of this book.
- Take the **GCSE Applied Business (Double Award)** by completing everything required for the Full GCSE, plus sitting an exam on Business Finance and completing two more Controlled Assessments on two of the following topics:
  ○ People in Business
  ○ Marketing and Customer Needs
  ○ Enterprise.
  These additional topics are covered in another book, *AQA Business for GCSE: Applied Business (Double Award)*.

NB This book covers the National Criteria for Business, on which all business GCSE courses are based, so it will be equally useful for GCSE courses other than AQA.

Getting the most out of this book

The book is divided into six sections. Section 1 provides key information about businesses, markets and the nature of enterprise. Sections 2 to 5 then reflect the AQA GCSE specification requirements: Starting a Business, Marketing, Finance, People in Businesses and Operations Management. You don't have to study the course in this order: that's up to you and your teacher.

Each chapter is designed to be approached in the same way:

- **Read** the 'In the News' section so that you have put the ideas into context, and can think about how they apply to the real world
- **Read** the text explaining the ideas
- **Read** 'Core Knowledge' and 'And More' which give the basic information and then further knowledge about the ideas in the chapter
- **'Have a Go'** at the exercises and activities to see how well you have understood the material. You can come back to the activities at any time if you need to revise the topic for tests or examinations, or you need to refresh your memory for Controlled Assessments.

How to use this book   vii

IN THE NEWS

Each chapter starts with a short news piece, based on recent events or a situation that puts the ideas discussed in the chapter into a real-world context.

This is followed by links to current websites and e-learning materials, so that the story can be followed up or investigated further, or so that additional information can be found.

After the news piece, the key information needed for the chapter is explained.

Summary

- This set of bullet points summarises the most important information contained in the chapter. You could think of this as the absolute minimum that you should learn from the chapter.

Core knowledge

The Core Knowledge then gives the basic knowledge that all students will need regarding this topic.

And more

Following on from the Core Knowledge, And More provides higher level or more in-depth knowledge for students who are aiming at higher grades or just want to improve their knowledge of a particular area.

Did you know...

These boxes are scattered throughout the book. They contain extra information that is either useful or interesting, and which can often help to put the topic into a real-world context.

Have a go!

This section contains a set of activities and exercises that can be carried out in class or at home in study time. Some are designed to be carried out on your own, others with friends or by using web resources.

AQA BUSINESS FOR GCSE: SETTING UP A BUSINESS

Group activity

The group activity is designed to be used with the group that you work with in school or college. It is not usually possible for this activity to be carried out by a single person, though sometimes a pair of people might complete the exercise. Often it is a way to gather a wider sample of opinions or skills than you have on your own, or to test your opinions against those of others.

Discussion

The discussion may follow on directly from the group activity, perhaps so that you can explore why you did or did not agree, had different views, or had different experiences to share. It will make you think more deeply about the area that you are studying!

Web-based activity

This activity requires access to a computer and an internet connection. It may take you to a specific site or sites, perhaps to see how an idea or knowledge has been put into practice in the real world, or it may ask you to use a search engine to find out more information. There is then a short activity based on what you have found.

Quickfire questions

These questions appear in every chapter. They will test your knowledge of the ideas and information in the chapter. Your teacher might use them to start or end a lesson, as a quiz with the class, or may ask you to complete them on your own. They are usually simple questions with simple answers, designed to check basic knowledge so, for instance, they might ask for definitions and brief explanations.

Hit the spot

> These questions require longer answers, where you can demonstrate your understanding of ideas and information in greater depth.

>> The chevrons (>) show the difficulty levels of the questions. One chevron is used for easier questions, that everyone should be able to do; two chevrons indicate harder questions, where some explanation of the answer is needed. The hardest questions, which may require you to state and justify an opinion, or to weigh up two sides of an argument, have three chevrons.

Cracking the code

Some words in the text are highlighted. These terms are explained under the 'Cracking the Code' heading. In business studies many words have a particular meaning, and it may even be different to how you use the word in normal speech. Cracking the Code will help you to use these words and terms in the correct way.

Acknowledgements

Every effort has been made to trace the copyright holders of quoted material. The publishers apologise if any sources remain unacknowledged and will be glad to make the necessary arrangements at the earliest opportunity. The authors and publishers would like to thank the following for permission to reproduce copyright photos:

aberystwyth/Alamy, p. 110; Action Press/Rex Features, p. 85; Adrian Sherratt/Alamy, p. 116; Alan Curtis/Alamy, p. 169; © Andrew Winning/Reuters/Corbis, p. 129; Banana Stock/Photolibrary Group, p. 155; Barking Dog Art, p. 50 (bottom); © BBC, p. 73; © Boris Ryaposov/iStockphoto.com, p. 33; BP, p. 2; Business Active, p. 104; © Chad Anderson/iStockphoto.com, p. 123; Christopher Furlong/Getty Images, p. 92; Clark's Pet Couriers, p. 98; Coffee Nation, p. 34; Colin Palmer Photography/Alamy, p. 144; Colin Underhill/Alamy, p. 20; The Franchise Magazine, p. 23; courtesy of Fraser Doherty, p. 14; funkyfood London – Paul Williams/Alamy, p. 150; Ian Shaw/Alamy, p. 124; Imagesource/Photolibrary Group, p. 165; Innocent Drinks, p. 50 (top); iStockphoto.com, title page; © malcolm romain/iStockphoto.com, p. 91; mediablitzimages (uk) Limited/Alamy, p. 27; Mike Webster/Rex Features, p. 26; © mipan – Fotolia.com, p. 61; Natasha Japp/iStockphoto.com, p. 55; Nick Hanna/Alamy, p. 160; Nick Randall/Rex Features, p. 79; © Patryk Galka/iStockphoto.com, p. 1; Photodisc, pp. 17, 38, 135, 139, 140, 149; PlayPumps International, p. 7; The Prince's Trust, p. 49; Robert Stainforth/Alamy, p. 68; Somos Images/Photolibrary Group, p. 40; Sonny Meddle/Rex Features, p. 134; Wayne Linden/Alamy, p. 62.

The photo on p. 2 is printed with kind permission of BP. The photo on p. 98 is printed with permission of Clark's Pet Couriers.

DEFINING BUSINESS AND ENTERPRISE

SECTION 1

Chapter 1
What is business?

IN THE NEWS

Without business, you would not be reading this book, or living in a house, travelling by bus or car, listening to music or wearing fashion. You would not be warm, or fed, or clothed. Business provides all of these goods and services and ranges from the tiniest, one person business, to huge multinationals with greater wealth than many countries.

In March 2008, the Duke and Duchess of York both appeared in the newspapers, both working with businesses. The Duke of York, in his role as a 'business ambassador' for the UK government, was visiting Indonesia to inspect BP's new natural gas plant in Bintuni Bay. The Duchess of York was involved in a reality TV show, trying to show people on low incomes how to eat more healthily. The Duke was visiting BP, a global oil and fuels company. The Duchess was encouraging people to buy from local producers, markets and stalls.

BP has operations and bases in about 100 countries, in every continent, from Austria, Algeria and Australia to Venezuela, Vietnam and Zambia. Its turnover approaches $300,000,000,000 a year and its profit almost $30,000,000,000. A typical fruit and vegetable market stall is tiny, with no employees, operating in one spot in one town. It may take £1000 a week, giving it a turnover of about £50,000, with profits of £15,000.

So what do they both share that makes them a business? Each provides something, and it is willing to sell to someone, who is willing to buy. Each provides either a good or service, or a combination of goods and services, to consumers in a market. Each tries to provide the good or service at a profit – in other words, they try to make more out of the sale of a product than it costs them to buy or make it. Businesses are involved in supplying goods and services to a market. BP supplies oil, gas and energy services to a market that is global in scope. A fruit and vegetable stall supplies food to a group of local customers. Each has costs that it must try to meet, and revenue from sales with which it must try to meet them. Each is at risk of failure if its business model does not work. (Big businesses have the chance of failing, just as much as small businesses, it's just more visible when they do!)

BP's new natural gas plant in Bintuni Bay

@ BP's background is at:
www.bp.com/extendedsectiongenericarticle.do?categoryId=5&contentId=70144157

The Duchess of York's show is at:
http://entertainment.timesonline.co.uk/tol/arts_and_entertainment/tv_and_radio/article3492502.ece

Statistics on small businesses may be found at:
www.statistics.gov.uk/cci/nugget.asp?id=11

What is business?

> **Did you know...**
> 'Needs' are those things that people need to survive, so don't include iPods, trainers, hair products or many other things that teenagers claim to 'need'!

Why do businesses exist?

A long time ago people saw to their own needs by providing for themselves. They recognised the sort of things that they needed – food, shelter, clothing, protection from the weather – they then provided these for themselves in order to survive. They collected water from streams and lakes. They grew or hunted their own food, and prepared it themselves. They made clothes from animal skins. They built their own shelters or lived in natural shelter.

Early societies provided for their own needs

Barter

At some point, people realised that certain people were better at some jobs than others. They decided that it would be better to let them do the jobs at which they were more efficient. So those who hunted best, hunted; those who were good at farming, looked after fields and animals, those who could build good shelters specialised in this. What this meant was that people were able to meet their needs more efficiently, and trade skills to make their lives better. This is called specialisation. At first, they just swapped the goods that they produced, or exchanged skills – a system known as barter. Later, when a way to measure value was invented (called 'money') they were able to carry out complicated transactions. Anyone who produced more of something than they needed was able to trade it for something they needed but did not have. This more efficient system also meant that people could trade for things that they did not need, but wanted. So production was not limited to food, clothes and shelter, but expanded not just to different types of clothes and different types of food but also to areas such as entertainment and leisure.

Profit

Businesses add value in order to make a product. They take a set of inputs (such as raw materials, say wheat) add value through a process (such as milling and baking) and produce an output (such as flour or bread). They add up the costs of all the inputs, then try to set a price that covers the costs and rewards them for their efforts. The

> **Did you know...**
> Not everyone is as well off as we are in the UK. Much of the world still survives at what is called 'subsistence' level. This means that they barely have enough to live on. Their 'needs' may be met, but there is little left over for any 'wants'.

AQA BUSINESS FOR GCSE: SETTING UP A BUSINESS

money they receive from sales is called revenue. If revenue is greater than cost, this is called profit.

Business and production

There are two main classes of products. One is goods – these are things that we can touch and hold. The other is services. In olden times, these were things like milling wheat, shoeing horses, being defended from enemies. Nowadays they include banking, insurance and communication. Production is the process that a good or service goes through in order to be made and sold.

- **Primary** production is the first stage, when raw materials are farmed, quarried or extracted. It includes industries like mining, farming, fishing and companies like BP.
- **Secondary** production is when the raw materials are turned into finished products or component parts of products. Businesses in this sector are called manufacturing or processing businesses. BP also operates in this sector, refining oil.
- **Tertiary** businesses provide services so that other businesses can operate efficiently. In this sector you will find insurance, transport, distribution (getting the goods to shops and customers), advertising, marketing, banking and finance. BP distributes and sells petrol, and advertises and markets itself, so it operates here as well. The market stall operates a service, so is in this sector.

Changes

The most important sectors to the UK economy are manufacturing and service, in particular the service sector. One in every five jobs in the UK is now in the financial and business sector, more than twice as many as ten years ago (see link). At the same time manufacturing businesses have been in decline over the past 20 years, as competition from overseas has been able to make goods more efficiently.

Primary, secondary and tertiary businesses

Did you know...

Britain's labour force has seen many changes over the past 20 years. A major change is the increase in the number and types of jobs carried out by women. In 1981, there were 3.2 million more men in work than women. Now the numbers are almost equal, with men performing 12.8 million jobs and women 12.7 million.

What is business?

Summary

- People have to satisfy their needs
- If they can do this efficiently, they can move on to wants
- Business provides goods and services that people need and want
- Businesses operate in markets
- Markets are where buyers and seller together agree a price for a quantity of goods or services
- Many businesses are in business to make a profit

Core knowledge

Most people would say that the reason businesses are in business is to make a profit and they would be right. But although profit may be at the heart of much business activity, it is not the only reason for businesses to exist. Before a small business can decide what is, or is not, profit, it needs to add in the hours that the owners have put in. Many small businesses fail to do this and look profitable, whereas owners might be better off working for someone else.

Businesses have a number of different aims, as you will see in Chapter 5, some of which are linked to profit and some to wider or different targets. Before a small business can decide what is, or is not, profit, it needs to add in the hours that the owners have worked. Many small businesses fail to do this, which makes them look profitable, when in reality the owners might be better off working for someone else. Someone might set up a business because they want to provide a certain service, they might want the independence of working for themselves, they might just like the thrill of taking a risk and may not be too bothered about the consequences.

Some enterprises use a business model in order to provide benefits to society, or parts of society. These are called social enterprises, and include charities and cooperatives. Social enterprise is defined by the government as having 'social objectives, whose surpluses are ... reinvested for that purpose in the business or the community, rather than being driven by the need to maximise profit'. What this means is that 'profit' is not for owners, but for the good of the community or to help the business grow so that it can do more good. There are around 55,000 social enterprises, with an annual turnover between them of almost £30 billion. There are some well-known names that are social enterprises ranging from *The Big Issue* and Jamie Oliver's Fifteen to the Co-operative Group, Café direct, Glas Cymru (Welsh Water) and The Eden Project.

And more

Businesses find out what people want and need – this is called demand – and then supply the goods and services to meet this demand. 'Needs' are the basic things required for survival, such as food, water and shelter; anything beyond this is a 'want'. Businesses have to make sure that goods and services are available at the right time, in the right place and at a price that people – consumers – are willing to pay. Goods and services are both 'products'. All that this means is that they are the result of a production process. This means that certain 'inputs' have been combined in a 'process' in order to produce certain 'outputs'. Inputs include raw materials, power and energy and people's labour. Processes include manufacturing,

processing, sorting, construction and refining. Different combinations of inputs and processes will produce different outputs. For example:
- A combination of knowledge, skill and labour could produce a haircut
- A combination of wood, graphite and machinery could produce a pencil
- A combination of metals, rubber, technology, machinery, energy and labour could produce a car

Products may be either goods or services. A good is something that can be touched and used. Sometimes goods are 'consumables'. This means that they are quickly used up and cannot be used again. Examples include items such as soap and shampoo and all food and drink. Other goods are more lasting and are called consumer 'durables'. These can be used many times over without really losing value. Examples of these include refrigerators, washing machines, dishwashers and freezers (so-called 'white' goods), cars, furniture, tools, household goods and machinery of all sorts. Services are provided to individuals and organisations and cannot be touched. Examples include transport, insurance and education, and personal services such as haircuts and manicures.

Have a go!

Group activity

Make a list of all the skills that you have in your group. Examples could include writing, speaking, drawing, spelling, sewing, painting, playing an instrument, cooking, remembering stuff, being a good footballer, swimming, etc., etc. If more than one person has the same skills, then rank them, or subdivide the skill so, while one swimmer might be faster, the other might have more stamina. When you have a list of skills, rank them in order of the ones you think are most useful to your survival.

Would your group survive as a society?

Do you think that you could exchange skills with another group to help survival?

Discussion

Are some skills more important than others? Discuss why this might be the case, or in what circumstances a skill might become useful. What are the skills that entertainers and sportspeople have that make them worth so much? Are these skills any use in helping with survival?

Web-based activity

Businessman Duncan Goose quit his city job to ride round the world on a motorbike. On his travels, he saw the real hardship caused to the people who do not have clean drinking water. One billion people do not have the basic 'need' of clean water. Two million die each year from dirty-water-related diseases. He set up bottled water company One, and ploughed all the profits into providing clean water in developing countries. The profits are used to build PlayPumps in remote areas. Basically, these are roundabouts that, when kids play on them, pump clean water up from below the surface. 'We can't change the world overnight, but we can improve the life of one person, one day at a time' is the motto of the company. Visit the websites below and then answer the questions.

What is business?

www.execdigital.co.uk/Driven-to-Drink—Duncan-Goose-talks-about-One-Water,-PlayPumps-and-social-entrepreneurship-_5860.aspx

www.beaconfellowship.org.uk/biography2007_dgoose.asp

Many businesses are set up for profit. Explain Duncan Goose's reason for setting up One. Do you think that this is a better model than a profit-based business? Give reasons for your views.

The One Water Playpump

Quickfire questions

1. What is a need?
2. What is a want?
3. What is meant by specialisation?
4. What is barter?
5. What is the difference between a good and a service?
6. What is meant by consumer durable?
7. What is primary production?
8. What is secondary production?
9. What is tertiary production?
10. What is a social enterprise?

Hit the spot

- Give two reasons why someone might want to specialise.
- Explain the input-process-output model, with at least one example.
- Give three reasons why someone might want to set up in business. Choose which you think is the best reason. Justify your choice.

Cracking the code

Business Providing products that people want, usually for profit. Learn this, it is a word that is commonly misspelt!

Primary 'First' – the first stage of production: extraction, quarrying, farming, mining, etc.

Secondary 'Second' – the second stage of production: manufacturing, refining, processing, etc.

Tertiary 'Third' – the third stage of production: i.e. the provision of services and support.

Chapter 2
The nature of markets

IN THE NEWS

Not long before you were born a loaf of bread (the government uses a standard 800 gram loaf for comparisons) cost just 50p. In February of 2007, according to *The Grocer* magazine, it topped £1 for the first time. By 2008 it had continued to rise and, even though cheaper and 'own brand' bread could be had, the cost for a 'normal' loaf was close to £1.20. Pasta, too, has been on the rise, with 500 g of pasta shapes costing up to £2, almost twice as much as ten years ago. Such price rises are important to us when they involve foods that are a staple part of our diet – things that we shop for on a regular basis. We are particularly affected when the price of a basic ingredient goes up. In this case, the price of bread and pasta is closely linked to the main ingredient in their manufacture – flour – and flour is made from wheat. Wheat is also a basic ingredient for some types of beer, for cereals and for pastry.

The price of wheat more than doubled in the year up to Spring 2008, when it hit $12.00 a bushel (the weight used to measure wholesale wheat – 60 lb. or approximately 27 kilos). As recently as October 2006 it had been less than $5.00 but, as demand has risen and supply been reduced, prices have continued to rise. The demand for wheat from growing nations like China and India has hit the market at the same time as bad weather has destroyed crops in Argentina and India. Even Canada, with its hundreds of miles of rolling wheat fields, has been hit by bad weather. In addition, there has been a new source of demand, as wheat (and products that can be grown instead of wheat) are harnessed for biofuels.

Higher prices may take a while to work their way through into every wheat-based product as big food businesses like Kellogg's and Kraft will have long-term supply contracts. But consumers are already not being offered bread with soup in restaurants, and prices of pizzas and pasta have risen. But what causes prices to rise (and sometimes fall), and how do these changes affect businesses?

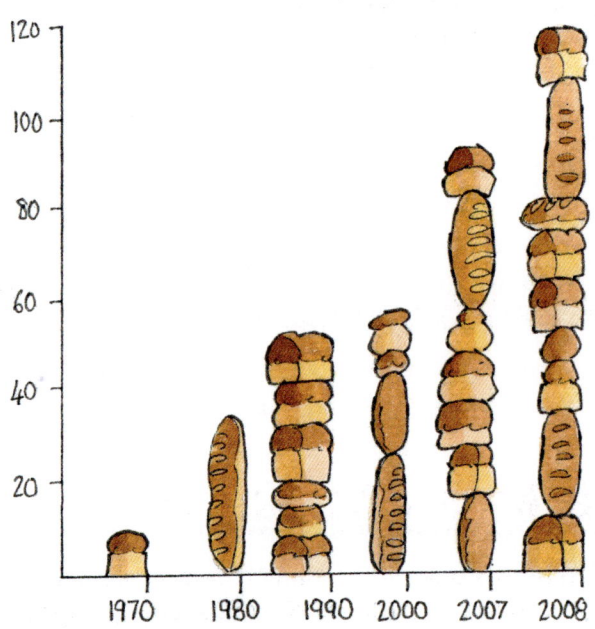

Changes in bread prices

@ Go to **statistics.gov.uk** for the latest information about prices – search for 'inflation' and 'retail price index'.
The Intellectual Property Office at **www.ipo.gov.uk/whatis.htm** tells you how a business can protect ideas, designs and trademarks.

The nature of markets

> **Did you know...**
> That China and America are neck and neck in the race to be the world's biggest market for Internet users, each with over 200 million users. China is rapidly catching America, however, and will continue to grow even after it has passed US numbers.

> **Did you know...**
> That there is enough food (of all types) to feed everyone in the world – the real problem is distribution, i.e. getting it from the people who can grow it to the people who need it.

Market map for Kellogg's cereals

```
                         KIDS
                          |
                          |  No Problemos
            Tiger Power   |    Eat My Shorts
                          | Coco Pops
                          |
                          |    Frosties
         Ricicles         |
HEALTH ───────────────────┼─────────────────── FUN
                          |
                          |  Crunchy Nut
                   Start  |
           Just Right     |
                          |    Crispix
              Special K   |
         All-Bran  Fruit'n Fibre
         Original      Cornflakes
                          |
                         ADULT
```

Markets and prices

All businesses operate in markets. A market is any way by which buyers and sellers are brought together. Sometimes this is physical – an actual place, like a farmers' market, Saturday market or craft fair. A supermarket is just a very large market, where any number of goods (and services) are offered for sale. Sometimes the market takes place 'virtually'. Buyers and sellers meet over a telephone connection, or via computer. In an auction market, people making telephone bids from abroad are still taking part in the market. Someone buying shares via a website and internet connection is still taking part in the stock market. New technology has opened up many more markets, and many more ways for people to operate businesses (and some more problems, as we shall see later). Prices in a market are determined by the number of people who want to buy and the number who want to sell. The amount people want to buy is called **demand**. The amount sellers want to sell is called **supply**.

Price changes

If too many sellers enter a market, then there will be too much supply. If every farmer saw that the price of wheat had gone up, and switched to wheat production, what do you think would happen to the price? If there are many buyers in a market, and it is not easy to increase supply, then the price will be pushed up. What do you think happens to the price of concert or Cup Final tickets if everyone wants one but there are only so many seats? The way that markets operate is to find the price where buyers and sellers agree on the amount to be exchanged.

Importance to businesses

This is vital to businesses because they all operate in markets. Some are highly competitive – in other words, there are a lot of other businesses trying to reach the same customers. In some cases markets are much less competitive. If you are the only person who supplies something, and it's something people want, you can probably ask a very high price.

Competition

In a competitive market, businesses can try to attract customers in a number of ways. The main two ways may be defined as

- **price competition** – where the business attracts customers by setting a particular price;
- **non-price competition** – where the business uses other means such as promotions and special offers or competes by providing extra or better services.

In some markets, there is very little competition. If someone has a good idea for a new product, they can actually protect it from competition by using things like patents, trademarks and copyright. In other markets, a few businesses may have grown large by taking over other businesses, and therefore getting rid of the competition. Sometimes they even have enough power to prevent other businesses from setting up in competition with them. In the interests of fairness, governments sometimes intervene in markets to provide goods or services that people would be unwilling or unable to pay for, or to try to make markets more competitive.

Mass or niche

Some markets are huge and are called mass markets. For example, millions of cars are sold every day, all over the world. Some markets are tiny and are called niche markets. A limited edition, special model of a particular car will have a very small market (and be very expensive). Some businesses will try to attract as many customers as possible, some will be happy to attract just a few customers, but with a highly-priced item.

Gaps in the market

Businesses look for changes and gaps in the market. Businesses can try to create a gap in the market, or they can try to find a gap, and fill it with a product. Alternatively, they could expand into other markets. Kellogg's could, for example, look for products that are not wheat-based to

A product for a niche market

bolster its range. Or it could move into completely different markets, like chocolate, or car production. (This is not as far-fetched as it sounds – Mars, for example, make pet food, coffee and pasta sauce, as well as being a leading confectionery firm.)

> **Did you know...?**
> That one of the fastest growing crime areas is identity theft. Protect yourself by using complex passwords, changing passwords often and by not using public machines for secure transactions.

Summary

- All businesses operate in markets
- Prices in a market are set by how many people want something, and how many people are willing to supply it
- Prices move up or down as supply and demand changes
- In some markets there is a lot of competition, in others, very little
- Businesses compete in markets by charging different prices, or through non-price competition
- Markets may be very large (mass) or very small (niche)
- Businesses try to change market conditions to their own advantage

Core knowledge

All businesses operate in markets. In a market, price is set by how many people want a good or service, and how many will supply it. Buyers will want something because they have a need for it – we have already come across this idea. But they can also be persuaded that they have a 'need'. Businesses will try to persuade customers through advertising, promoting and branding. One method is to find a gap in the market or, if there is no gap, to create one by creating desire and therefore demand for a product.

Kellogg's brand strength lies in its most popular cereal products. Kellogg's could try various ways to sell more of these. It could lower price, it could increase advertising or it could promote the products in other ways. Also, Kellogg's could bring out new products to cover those areas where it doesn't feel it is strong. To do this, it can draw up a '**market map**'. This divides the market into four, with each part showing one part of the market at which a product might be aimed. One of the skills of market mapping, for a business, is to be able to define the key parts of their market. These could, for example, be men, women, young or old people, luxury products or everyday necessities, low- or high-priced products, healthy or 'indulgent' products, and so on. You can see from Kellogg's market map that they market their range at both young and old, and have some products whose strength is their 'healthy' message, while others are strong because they are more 'fun'. 'Fun' products are, of course, one way to get young people to eat healthily. You can see that adult, healthy cereals are very strong, with Kellogg's cornflakes central to this. The two Bart Simpson brands (top right quarter) have been added in the last few years to strengthen this part of the market. There is still, however, quite a gap in the market for a 'fun' product for adults. Kellogg's could move Crunchy Nut more in that direction (by advertising), or come up with another product to fill this gap.

AQA BUSINESS FOR GCSE: SETTING UP A BUSINESS

And more

Many markets now take place 'virtually', i.e. with the buyer and seller never meeting. This has opened up a lot of new opportunities for businesses. Businesses can use new technology to advertise products and to provide ways for people to buy. Most businesses now have a website operation, which will include ways to order products. Many small businesses are run using websites like eBay and using protected payment systems like PayPal.

Of course, the major problem with a technology-based market, is that you do not meet the person from whom you are buying/to whom you are selling, so the exchange and payment cannot take place at the same time. If you think about a normal, non-technology-based transaction, you often hand over your money at the same time as you receive the goods. Sometimes there is a delay, particularly in business-to-business (B2B) transactions, while orders are made (purchase orders), deliveries are made and paper requests for payment (invoices) follow, but even this process is nowadays often electronic and therefore much faster. There is also the growing problem of fraud and identity theft. There are ways to reduce these problems – for example by using a third party to hold funds until goods are delivered (this is how PayPal works), by using secure servers and by having good firewalls. Nevertheless, e-crime is a growth area.

Technology helps businesses in other ways. There is now little need for businesses to handle large amounts of cash (and many businesses now even refuse to take cheques) as transfers can be made safely and efficiently by **EFTPOS** and chip and pin cards. Businesses can also collect a lot of information on customers and their buying habits, through data gathered at electronic checkouts.

Have a go!

Group activity

Make a list of the top five advertising campaigns that are taking place at the moment. Compare your list with other members of your group and decide on an agreed top five. For each campaign, say what you think the business is trying to do. Is it trying to enter a new market or expand an existing one? Perhaps it is just trying to reposition a product in a different market segment. Rank the businesses according to which you think have the most effective advertising.

Discussion

Discuss the reasons why you think your chosen advertisers have decided to go in this direction. What do you think is happening to the market in each of the cases at which you have looked that would make the business try this particular tactic? Do you agree with them or could you recommend another course of action?

The nature of markets 13

Web-based activity

Biofuels are an area where there is some argument. Some people say that they are putting up the price of wheat (and other foods) so that poor people cannot afford food. Other people say that there are benefits to the environment that outweigh any problems. Use a search engine to find out about biofuels and decide if you are for or against them. Put together a folder, poster or display that supports your argument.

Quickfire questions

1. What is a market?
2. What forces in a market determine price?
3. What is a 'virtual' market?
4. In which two ways do businesses compete?
5. How could a new business protect itself against competition?
6. What is a mass market?
7. What is a niche market?
8. What is a gap in a market?
9. What is a 'market map'?
10. What is meant by 'identity theft'?

Hit the spot

> Give an example of a competitive market. Describe the features that make it competitive.

>> Explain why non-price competition might be the main way to compete in a highly competitive market.

>>> Suggest three possible problems with markets and new technology. Evaluate ways to limit these problems.

Cracking the code

Demand The amount people want to buy.

EFTPOS (Electronic Funds Transfer at Point of Sale) Moving funds directly from one account to another (e.g. your bank to a shop's bank).

Market mapping A way of dividing the market into key areas.

Non-price competition Using ways other than price to compete.

Price competition Setting a different price to your competitors.

Supply The amount that producers/businesses want to sell.

Chapter 3
Taking risks – enterprise

IN THE NEWS

Superjam

SuperJam

Fraser Doherty decided, at the age of 14, that he would like to make some extra pocket money. Looking around, he saw that many boys and girls of the same age group as himself were working long hours at jobs that were anything but rewarding. In fact, the figures show that a third of under-16s hold down a part-time job, with the most popular being car washing and newspaper deliveries. Once over 16, they can earn more by waiting tables, babysitting or shop work. None of this attracted Fraser, however, so he decided to look around for other opportunities. With the help of his grandmother, he began to produce jam, finding a ready local market in friends and neighbours. Market research showed him that jam was a market in decline, but only because it was seen as such an unhealthy product. His grandmother's wartime jams had contained a minimum of sugar – due to shortages – so used other ingredients to produce sweetness. Fraser's jams are sweetened with grape juice, making them much healthier. In addition, everyone, he thought, does strawberry and blackberry, so I'm going to try something different. He experimented with different fruits and produced many more unusual jams, concentrating on the so-called 'superfruits' such as cranberries and blueberries and ingredients such as ginger. Friends and neighbours spread the word and sales rapidly increased. Fraser found himself selling at farmers' markets and to delicatessens as demand grew.

By the time he was 16, Fraser was producing 1000 jars a week, as demand rocketed after appearances on the UK Food Channel, BBC TV's Working Lunch and C4's Tricky Business.

In early 2007 Fraser gained a huge order from national supermarket chain Waitrose. He had to say goodbye to the home kitchen and set up proper production facilities in order to supply most of Waitrose's 183 stores. In October, giant retailer Tesco took up further supply.

Current success, however, is built on immense hard work and long hours. A teenager's social life was sacrificed for 60-hour weeks making jam and weekends spent selling it at farmers' markets, often with little success when bad weather kept customers indoors. Early losses and setbacks, however, just made Fraser more determined to get the product and the market right.

The result? Fraser is well on his way to becoming Scotland's first jam millionaire!

www.realbusiness.co.uk
http://news.Scotsman.com
www.bbc.co.uk/dragonsden/

> **Did you know...?**
>
> There are now over 400,000 millionaires in the UK and just ten British billionaires! Britain's richest person is a Russian – Chelsea FC owner Roman Abramovich is worth £7.5 billion.

Enterprise

Fraser has shown the qualities of an **entrepreneur** and of **enterprise**. These are both words that you will come across often in your study of business because what they represent is so central to the success of a business. Enterprise means taking risks and developing new ideas. It means finding the money to try products and ideas out on the market. Without enterprise, and without entrepreneurs, there would be no new business ideas. Without entrepreneurs we would have no electricity, no motor cars, no air travel, no computers (or computer games), no mobile phones ... The invention of each of these is not enough to ensure its success. Each needed an entrepreneur – a person who was willing to take a risk and hope that people would buy the product. Take the motor car, for example. Without Henry Ford's idea of factory-led mass production, the car would probably still be a luxury item for the very few. He didn't invent the car, but he did make sure that ordinary people could afford to buy it.

Enterprise therefore involves:

- *New ideas*: Entrepreneurs think of new products, of new ways to use old products, or new markets to which they can sell products. The key ideas of the entrepreneur are to do with bringing products to market.

- *Money*: To do this, entrepreneurs need money – in business we call this finance – in order to develop products, test products, make changes to products and tell people about products (and all the good things about them). They may need to set up production, for instance in a factory. They may need to employ people (who will then want paying). They may need to buy **raw materials** before they can start making a product. Many entrepreneurs do not have enough of their own money, so have to convince other people of the value of their product. Sometimes they may borrow money. Sometimes they may persuade other people or organisations to risk money on their idea.

- *Risk*: Entrepreneurs risk their own money, other people's money, and their own reputations. Taking a risk is probably the hardest part of enterprise. The entrepreneur must be prepared to lose – and then to try again.

- *Reward:* Of course this is what drives all entrepreneurs. Seeing a product on sale and being used may be reward enough. But the reward that most entrepreneurs seek is profit. This means making more in **revenue** than it costs to produce the product.

Qualities of an entrepreneur

The typical qualities of an entrepreneur are a bit like those of an old-time explorer. They must really believe that they can succeed and, as well, must be:

- *Willing to take advice*: Entrepreneurs need to listen to people who can help them. This may be professional advice, such as from a bank or marketing company. It may be advice from

> **Did you know...?**
>
> Market analysts Datamonitor say that women now make up 46 per cent of the UK's millionaires. Singer Charlotte Church became Britain's youngest millionaire in 2004 at the age of just 14.

AQA BUSINESS FOR GCSE: SETTING UP A BUSINESS

Entrepreneurs take risks …

friends and colleagues. It may be advice from customers about the product that the entrepreneur is selling.

- *Enthusiastic*: Entrepreneurs need energy and enthusiasm. This is linked to self-belief. They must really believe in the product that they are selling and be keen to persuade people to buy it.

- *Hard working*: Entrepreneurs cannot afford to be lazy. They are risking both their own money and, often, that of other people. Often success means putting in long hours. (Look at the 60-hour weeks Fraser had to put in on top of anything else he wanted to do, like socialise or study.)

- *Persistent*: (meaning 'keeps on trying'). This is really important. Entrepreneurs will not always have a smooth ride. They will encounter many obstacles and have to face setbacks as well as enjoy successes. To become a success, they must be prepared to keep trying.

Did you know…?

Many entrepreneurs started as really small businesses – Virgin's Richard Branson started with a student magazine; Bodyshop founder Anita Roddick with a single shop; Tesco started in 1924 when founder Jack Cohen combined the first two letters of his surname with the initials of TE Stockwell, from whom he bought a delivery of tea.

Summary

- Business relies on people with new ideas
- These new ideas can be turned into new products, or new uses for existing products
- People willing to test these ideas in the market are called entrepreneurs
- The quality that these people show is enterprise
- Enterprise involves many other qualities, such as hard work and enthusiasm

Core knowledge

All businesses start with new ideas. In general these can be split into two. First, completely new products, second, existing products, but aimed at a different part or segment of a market. Let's first understand the terms.

A *product* is the result of business activity. It can be either a good or a service. A good is a physical product like a car, a mobile phone, a bicycle, a computer game or a loaf of bread. A service is

Taking risks – enterprise 17

something that is done for a person or organisation like a haircut, a car service, insurance or transport. A taxi driver owns a product (the cab) and provides a service (the cab ride).

A *market* is anywhere where a product may be bought or sold. A traditional market (like a farmers' market) has stalls and stallholders offering goods for sale, but a car showroom is as much a market as this, and businesses like eBay show that a market can exist anywhere – even in cyberspace. Markets are broken down by businesses into smaller parts or segments, so that each segment can be more accurately targeted.

Enterprise may therefore involve:

- A completely new good. One inventor developed a glue that didn't stick very well. The entrepreneur in him turned it into the highly successful Post-it notes business.
- A completely new service. When personal music players first came out, a number of businesses were established to turn people's record collections into digital media.
- An improved or better good. Cars are a good example, many now have as standard airbags, electric windows, abs braking, lower carbon emissions, etc.
- An improved or better service. Silverjet saw that there was a demand for business class flights so launched an airline where all seats were business class. Unfortunately, like many new businesses, it failed!

The Post-it note was a completely new idea

And more

Modern successful entrepreneurs recognise that there are other vital qualities that they will need. Being a successful entrepreneur isn't just about taking risks, it is about being able to manage those risks. Risk management is the skill of judging how important or dangerous a risk is, and then making sure that it is minimised wherever possible. For example, there is much less risk involved in bringing a product to a small part of a market in order to test it than there is in trying to hit the whole possible market first. Many entrepreneurs therefore introduce ideas in small ways or small markets, just to test them out.

Success also involves the ability to solve problems. Problem-solving skills mean that the entrepreneur can see a way through difficulties that other people cannot. It means identifying the problem, coming up with possible solutions, deciding on the best solution (linked to risk management) and then putting the solution into effect.

Entrepreneurs must also have team-working skills. They must be able to get the best out of those around them, making good use of people's different qualities. As well as being able to lead teams, they must have good listening skills, and be prepared to act on advice given by team members.

Some entrepreneurs, having been successful, try to help other entrepreneurs by investing in them. This is called providing risk capital. Such entrepreneurs are also called venture capitalists. Watch any episode of the BBC programme *Dragons' Den* and you will meet successful entrepreneurs (the panel) and up-and-coming ones (those with ideas and products).

AQA BUSINESS FOR GCSE: SETTING UP A BUSINESS

Have a go!

Group activity

Working in a group, you are going to manage a risk. Think of an activity that you, or a group of friends, could undertake. This could be something simple like going to the cinema or travelling to the next town. It could be something more adventurous, like an outdoor pursuits weekend or even a trip abroad. Once you have decided, carry out a risk assessment on the activity. Break it down into small steps, decide what the risk is for each step and then say how this risk could be minimised. Finally, explain why such risk management is really important to businesses.

There is risk in the simplest action

Some activities are high risk

Discussion

What do you think is the single most important quality for an entrepreneur? Which entrepreneurs can you use as evidence to support your decision?

Web-based activity

Visit the BBC's website for *Dragons' Den* at **www.bbc.co.uk/dragonsden/**. Listen to the opening credits. These will tell you how the 'dragons' made their money. Then watch the first part of any of the 'pitches'. When the pitch is over, pause the broadcast and write down three of the sort of questions that you would ask. Decide what answers you would like to hear, then decide whether you would be 'in' or 'out' with this particular entrepreneur. Then play the rest of the broadcast to see what the dragons asked and decided.

Taking risks – enterprise

Quickfire questions

1. What is the business quality shown by the entrepreneur?
2. What do entrepreneurs take? What do they develop?
3. What was Henry Ford's winning idea?
4. Entrepreneurs can bring new products to market. How else can they make products successful?
5. Define revenue.
6. Define profit.
7. Give three key qualities of an entrepreneur.
8. Suggest two sources of professional advice for entrepreneurs.
9. Describe what is meant by venture capital.
10. Name one successful entrepreneur and suggest one factor that made him/her a success.

Hit the spot

> Give two reasons why a successful entrepreneur might support other entrepreneurs.

> Explain how important enterprise skills are to business.

> Which quality of an entrepreneur do you think is most important to success? Explain why you think this.

Cracking the code

Enterprise Taking risks and developing new ideas for successful businesses.

Entrepreneur The person who shows enterprise qualities.

Raw materials Basic material and components used to make a product (like wood used to make tables).

Revenue Money received by a business from sales.

Chapter 4
Reducing the risks of starting a business: Franchising

IN THE NEWS

What is the world's biggest fast-food franchise operation? McDonald's? Pizza Hut? Perhaps KFC? In fact, it is the hugely successful Subway chain, which makes its own bread daily and specialises in fresh ingredients and healthy alternatives. Subway – now not just the biggest fast-food franchise, but the biggest franchise operation of any sort in the world – started in 1965 when two friends decided to set up a sandwich-making enterprise. Once it was a success, they decided to expand. They could have done this by opening up new stores themselves but, instead, decided to franchise the idea.

In 2008 Subway opened its 28,000th store worldwide. By the middle of the year it had overtaken McDonald's in terms of the number of stores operating, opening them at a rate of almost one a day. The year before it had reached its thousandth store in Australia and its thousandth in Britain and Ireland when it opened three new franchises on the same day (in Manchester, Southend and Donegal, Ireland). It currently operates in 86 countries worldwide. Unlike many of its competitors, it is also experimenting with a different cultural 'mix' and offering sandwiches made according to religious and dietary rules such as halal and kosher. This will allow it access to even more markets in Asia and Africa.

Subway makes fresh sandwiches (in submarine-shaped rolls – hence the name) so has no need for fryers or grills, making it a more attractive proposition to many than its hot food competitors such as KFC, Burger King, Pizza Hut and McDonald's. Because it does not need cooking facilities, Subways have many more possible venues available to them than cooked food outlets and can be found in an enormous variety of venues, apart from the high street.

The world's biggest fast-food franchise

It has also been more easily able to adapt its menus to healthy eating, having no fried products and being able to substitute low fat and low calorie ingredients where possible. Its range of fresh sandwiches and salads now includes an 'under 6 g of fat' line that has become very popular. Part of the success is down to the levels of support available to franchisees. They receive advice from Subway consultants on all aspects of the operation, from choosing a site to training the staff and from buying in ingredients to marketing. The formula is so successful that many franchisees have opened multiple outlets.

@
www.subway.co.uk/about_latest_details.asp?press_news_id=32
www.thefranchisemagazine.net/
www.TheUKFranchiseDirectory.net
www.FranchiseDirect.co.uk

Reducing the risks of starting a business: Franchising

> **Did you know...**
> Although there are many examples of fast-food franchises, not all franchises are in this area! The Body Shop, BSM (British School of Motoring) and Prontaprint are all franchise operations, as are many other well known high street businesses.

Franchises

Franchising is often classed as a type of business ownership. It is, however, a type of business organisation, rather than ownership. Franchises may be bought and sold by sole traders, partnerships, companies, cooperatives and charities. (One Subway branch, for example, is owned and operated by a church and sited in the church in Buffalo, New York, where it is part of a drive to help underprivileged kids by providing work opportunities.) A franchise is when a business sells the right to use its trade marks, brand, image, logo, etc. to another business. In effect, the buyer buys the right to trade using the successful ideas of another business.

How a franchise works

When a successful business decides that it would like to expand, it can do this in a number of different ways. It could, if it were a retail business, open more branches, or expand into internet sales. A manufacturing business could move into larger premises. Any business could expand by buying out its rivals. Alternatively, it can sell its successful business idea or format to others that want to profit from it.

The successful business that decides to expand in this way is called the **franchiser**. It sells the **franchise** to a **franchisee**. This will be for a certain sum of money called a **fee** (ranging from a few hundred to tens of thousands of pounds) plus, usually, a percentage share of the **turnover** or profits of the franchisee, called a **royalty**.

Franchisers may also gain by selling products to franchisees at higher prices than if they bought them elsewhere. There are advantages and disadvantages to both franchiser and franchisee.

Advantages of franchising

The franchiser

- is able to carefully select franchisees, and only sell to those who it thinks will add value to the brand;
- knows that franchisees, who have risked their own money, will be keen and enthusiastic to make the business a success;
- can expand more rapidly;
- receives money from the franchisee, so does not risk its own money on expansion;
- can gain from *economies of scale*, through being able to buy in bulk (one of the advantages of expansion).

The franchisee

- has had some of the financial hard work done in advance as the franchiser has a good idea of what setting up the business will cost, and reflects this in the franchise fee;
- receives support from the franchiser when setting up and ongoing support in terms of advice, marketing, advertising, etc. For Subway, this is reckoned to be one of its real strengths and includes financial, marketing and training advice.

> **Did you know...?**
> The word 'franchise' is often used to mean 'the right to' do something. For instance, the rights to broadcast Premiership Football matches, or Six Nations rugby internationals, are sold as 'franchises', as they are limited to a certain amount of time and then must be renegotiated (and paid for again).

Disadvantages of franchising

The franchisee

- may be restricted in terms of what they can do with the business. Some franchisers, for example, insist that they only sell their own brands, and that they only use certain suppliers. Subway is more flexible on this than many of its rivals;
- may feel that royalties are too high and they are not being rewarded for their effort;
- are unable to sell the franchise on without the agreement of the franchiser.

The franchiser

- is risking the business brand and reputation, and may end up with a franchisee that damages both.

A franchise, therefore, provides a safer route into business for many and a more certain route to expansion for many businesses.

The franchiser can offer advice and support

Did you know...

Some businesses take both routes to expansion – opening new branches themselves and franchising. McDonald's, for example, has both its own branch network and tens of thousands of franchised branches. Control over stock, cooking, training, service, etc. is such that you will never be able to tell which is franchised and which is not!

Summary

- A franchise is where a successful business expands by selling the right to use its business model
- The franchiser is the business selling the franchise
- The franchisee is the business buying the franchise
- Franchises are usually bought for a fee, plus a royalty
- Some advantages of franchising include, for the franchiser, easier expansion and more certain financial flows; for the franchisee, a successful model and lower risk
- Some disadvantages include, for the franchiser, the possibility of a franchisee damaging its reputation; for the franchisee, higher costs and restrictions on the business
- Statistically, franchises are more likely to succeed than other independent start-ups, so remain popular

Reducing the risks of starting a business: Franchising

Core knowledge

The process of franchising

Firstly, a business has to be a success. Secondly, it has to have a business model or type that will lend itself to franchising. A car manufacturer or oil refining business is unlikely to be able to attract franchisees. Costs and risks will be far too high. In addition, the franchiser needs to know that the franchise will add to his own business, rather than compete with it. If a car manufacturer were to sell a franchise, the cars produced would compete in the market with its own vehicles. A franchiser must therefore have a business model that

- can easily be transferred;
- does not cost too much to set up;
- can be kept from competing with itself or other franchisees.

This is why many franchise operations are found in the fast-food market. Premises are reasonably small and therefore easier to find. With Subway, they are even more flexible as frying facilities are not needed. Costs to set up can be kept at a competitive level. As with many franchises, exclusive areas can be given so that one franchise is not in competition with another.

The franchiser will advertise the availability of a franchise through one of the franchise magazines (such as *The Franchise Magazine*) or through a website, such as www.TheUKFranchiseDirectory.net or www.FranchiseDirect.co.uk

Franchisees can then see what it will cost to buy the franchise, the likely rewards, and the restrictions that the franchiser puts on the business. The franchiser will also be careful to vet applicants and many, who it does not think would be good for the image of the business, or where it is not convinced there is sufficient business knowledge, will be rejected. With a popular franchise, like Subway, there are often waiting lists of those who wish to apply.

And more

Comparing a franchise with an independent business

Although many people have the dream of starting their own business, few actually make it. Many people are put off by the risk of failure. Franchisees are buying a successful business idea, so there is less chance of failure. According to the Office for National Statistics (ONS) around 50 per cent of new businesses fail in the first two years of operation. For franchises, this figure plummets to less than 10 per cent. In addition, over 90 per cent of franchises are in profit – and stay that way. The British Household Panel Survey 2008, based on 6000 households, says that

AQA BUSINESS FOR GCSE: SETTING UP A BUSINESS

only one in seven of those who wish to start a business actually do and, although some will eventually make it, more than two-thirds never manage to realise their dream.

Standards

The franchisee must convince the franchiser that s/he has enthusiasm and business knowledge, and can run the business to the standards required. Once an application is accepted, the franchiser will then provide some or all of the stock, advertising (including national advertising for the brand, from which every outlet benefits), marketing and point of sale materials, financial advice, training, insurance, legal advice, design and shop fitting and even loans.

Both the commercial TV station and the product advertised are franchises

Other franchises

Not all franchise operations are in retail. Regional TV stations in the UK (commercial stations like TV South West and Yorkshire Television) buy a 'right to broadcast' in a particular area from the Independent Broadcasting Authority. Train companies like Virgin and National Express buy a franchise for the right to run trains on Network Rail's tracks.

Have a go!

Group activity

Visit your local High Street or shopping centre and map the shops that you find there. You should try to map between 20 and 30 shops. Now try to find out which are franchises. Divide the number of shops between the members of your group and, by using the internet, or by interviewing shop staff, find out which are franchises. Once you have put all the information together, produce a chart to show which are franchises.

Discussion

Discuss the reasons that you can give for these businesses being franchises. Which of them did you expect to be franchises (refer to the Core Knowledge on page 23)? Which of them were you surprised to find were franchises?

Reducing the risks of starting a business: Franchising   25

Web-based activity

Imagine that you had £10,000 to invest in a new business. Visit either **www.TheUKFranchiseDirectory.net** or **www.FranchiseDirect.co.uk** and decide which business you would like to buy. If you need more money, you could go into partnership with a classmate if you can persuade him or her that your idea is better than theirs!

Quickfire questions

1 Define 'franchise'.
2 Explain the difference between the franchiser and the franchisee.
3 What is a 'royalty'?
4 Name five fast food franchise operations.
5 Name five other franchise operations.
6 List five types of support that the franchiser might give to the franchisee.
7 Give three advantages of franchising to the franchiser.
8 Give three advantages of franchising to the franchisee.
9 Name at least three disadvantages, to either franchiser or franchisee.
10 Give three things a franchise needs for it to be a success.

Hit the spot

Outline what is meant by a franchise.

What is the difference between a royalty and a fee?

Explain whether you would rather have a royalty charged on turnover or profit, and why.

Give three benefits of a franchise to either the franchiser or the franchisee.

Give three drawbacks of a franchise to either the franchiser or the franchisee.

Explain why a franchise start-up might be a better bet than an independent business start-up.

Read the information on Subway. Which part of their business model is it that makes the franchise operation such a success? Give reasons for your answer.

Cracking the code

Fee The price of the franchise.
Franchise When a business sells the right to use its successful business model in order to expand.
Franchisee The person or business buying the franchise.
Franchiser The person or business selling the franchise.
Royalty In relation to franchises, a percentage of the turnover of the franchisee, paid to the franchiser.
Turnover The number of products sold times the price of each.

Chapter 5
Business aims and objectives

IN THE NEWS

Antonio Carluccio was surprised to receive an early seventieth birthday present when the Queen presented him with an honorary OBE. 'I didn't think an Italian citizen could get a British honour,' he said in a later interview. But Antonio shouldn't have been surprised at his award for 'services to hospitality' as he is one of the most successful chefs and restaurant owners of the past 20 years. At each stage of his business career, he has had clear aims and objectives – targets that he wanted to reach. Having reached these targets, Antonio then moved on to harder or higher objectives. As a successful chef in the 1990s, Antonio had found it frustrating that he could not obtain the fresh ingredients that he needed for the high quality food that he wanted to cook. He had been taught, in his childhood in Italy, to recognise the 'free' foods of the countryside such as berries, leaves and, especially, edible fungi such as mushrooms and truffles. He opened his first shop, with the aim of providing fresh ingredients, in 1991. The overall aim of the shop was 'to provide great quality, authentic Italian food at sensible prices. We also wanted to allow informal but excellent service to our customers.' Other aims have to be financial – obviously the shop had to survive and then, hopefully, make a profit. It did, and then growth became an aim as a wholesale business and other shops were opened. In November 1999 a new concept was launched when a combined food shop and 'caffè' was opened. These are restaurants with a food shop attached. Each restaurant is based on the idea that the ingredients are as important as the finished meal, so each has a specialist food shop attached to it where customers can buy the ingredients for the Italian dishes served. There is also a wide range of coffees. Carluccio's can now be found all around the country, and the company is quoted on AIM (AIM is the Alternative Investment Market, the little brother of the Stock Exchange). A further aim is to expand internationally, and the first shop outside the UK was opened in Dublin in 2008.

All through the process, however, the original aim – the 'mission statement' – has remained the same: good quality produce, authentic Italian food, sensible prices, excellent service. By staying true to this target, Carluccio's has continued to grow and thrive from its beginnings as a single shop run by a chef and his wife.

Chef and entrepreneur Antonio Carluccio

Business aims and objectives

- You can read the 'five minute interview' with Antonio Carluccio at www.independent.co.uk/news/people/the-5minute-interview-antonio-carluccio-chef-and-restaurateur-396967.html
- The Federation of Small Businesses has surveyed UK business to see who follows a policy of corporate social responsibility (CSR). Read the report at www.fsb.org.uk/data/default.asp?ID=82&loc=policy
- Go to the government's support site for businesses, called Business Link, and see what they have to say about acting responsibly being good for business. You will find the site at www.businesslink.gov.uk

Did you know...

Many small businesses are in business for reasons other than profit. A business may want to provide a service, or exist because the person running it prefers to work for himself or herself.

Aims and objectives

Both **aims** and **objectives** are types of target, so a business needs to distinguish between them. The aim of the business is usually defined as its long-term target. Sometimes these may be impossible to measure (Carluccio's 'excellent service', for example) or so far into the future that they may never be reached (Coca-Cola's aim is to be 'the beverage of choice' all around the world, replacing water, tea and coffee; Heinz's aim for its tomato ketchup is to be 'the world's favourite ketchup, on every table').

These aims may be stated as '**mission statements**' and, although they may not be attainable, give a good idea of what drives the business. The objectives of the business are the shorter-term targets that it hits on the way to its aim. They are like stepping stones on the way and can be further broken down into targets.

Did you know...

Businesses will try to quantify targets where possible. For instance, for customer service they will keep a record of the number of complaints and the speed with which they were resolved. They may also record if, and how often, a customer returns.

SMART targets

Targets are smaller steps, and need to be measurable so that progress can be seen. Businesses usually set themselves what are called SMART targets. These are:

- SPECIFIC – the target should be as definite as possible
- MEASURABLE – it should be quantifiable, so often involves figures or percentages
- ATTAINABLE – it should be a target that it is possible to reach
- RELEVANT – it should form a logical part of the overall strategy of the business
- TIME-RELATED – there should be a set time for the achievement of the target.

Types

Business objectives can, broadly speaking, be put into three categories:

- being satisfied
- wanting to reach a maximum
- wanting to reach a minimum.

For small businesses, in particular, the idea of 'being satisfied' as a target is a very common one. Many small-business owners are happy working for themselves, providing a certain level of service, or making a certain level of income. For them the idea of doing more, or of expanding, just means extra work. They are happy with what they have. Often one of the main objectives of a small business is to maintain its independence.

Maximising

The most commonly quoted 'maximum' that a business might want to reach is profit. This is the difference between costs and revenues. This is not, however, the only area that a business might wish to maximise. It could want to maximise:

- *Productivity* – to look for the maximum efficiency of its workers and machines and combinations of them;
- *Manpower* – to employ the best possible people, at the best rates;
- *Innovation* – to be the first to market, always at the cutting edge of technology;
- *Management expertise* – to make sure it has the most efficient and loyal managers with the highest levels of knowledge and training;
- *Marketing* – to have the biggest slice or most control over the market in which it operates;
- *Resources* – to use the most reliable sources and achieve the best value for money;
- **Social responsibility** – to have the best reputation of the business in the community.

Of course, any or all of these are likely to have the effect of making the business more efficient, or its products more desirable, and will therefore contribute to greater profitability.

Minimising

Minimising objectives are those where a business wants to make the least, rather than the most, of something. A firm might, for example, want to minimise **labour turnover** due to the expense of appointing and training new workers. They may want to have as small an impact on the environment as possible. Usually these can be turned into 'maximising' aims – such as labour efficiency or social responsibility.

Did you know...?

Social enterprises are likely to have targets that are not related to profit. They may, for example, want to bring the maximum benefit to a community, or to help as many people as possible. They are still, therefore, likely to have efficiency targets.

Business aims and objectives

Summary

- Businesses set themselves targets
- Aims are long-term targets
- Objectives are shorter-term targets, steps to reaching aims
- Targets should be SMART
- Targets are often set to maximise something
- Sometimes a business aims to make the 'least' of a negative target

Core knowledge

Aims and objectives may both be thought of as types of targets. Businesses need to measure whether or not they are succeeding in what they are doing, so need to set targets. Objectives are not just 'set' however. They need to be carefully thought out as the effort to achieve objectives is a key part of running a business. Businesses must decide which objectives are more important in terms of which will contribute most to the future of the business. The success of a business may be judged by how clear and appropriate its objectives are, and how successful it is in reaching them.

Businesses therefore need ways by which they can measure progress. Sometimes this is easy, as figures are involved. Sometimes it is much harder. How do you know, for example, that customer satisfaction has improved? One way is to turn these into SMART targets. Most small businesses will start with the main aim of surviving, only then can they look to the future. The business would want to break even (meaning that they earn in revenue at least as much as they have spent) or make a small profit. Many small enterprises do not want to expand once they have reached this point. Owners and other stakeholders (who are discussed in the following chapter) need to know what they are aiming for, and whether they are reaching it. The most common targets are

- *Profit* – usually measured as a percentage of turnover;
- *Growth* – for those businesses that want to expand either in their current market or into new markets;
- *Market share* – the bigger the share of the market owned by a business, the more power they have in that market;
- *Customer satisfaction* – do customers come back a second time, are complaints kept to a minimum, is feedback from customers good?

AQA BUSINESS FOR GCSE: SETTING UP A BUSINESS

> **And more**
>
> One area in which there has been growth in the past few years is that of corporate social responsibility. This (often shortened to CSR) has become a central part of the aims of many businesses. Businesses work in communities, they need supplies of labour or raw materials, they need to transport finished goods. CSR is all about carrying out these activities with as little negative impact as possible. Media interest in businesses making a profit on the back of child labour, or poorly paid and overworked third-world workers, led to a response by consumers. Businesses that damaged the communities in which they worked – environmentally or socially – or who underpaid suppliers, lost customers. In some cases, they also lost the support of their own investors. Many businesses have decided that it is better to act **ethically** than to maximise profit on the back of anti-social practice. They have therefore written into their corporate aims the idea of at least giving back to communities as much as they take out, treating workers fairly and being careful of their use of resources. There are a number of key areas that these policies cover:
>
> - *Fairtrade* – making sure that suppliers receive a fair price for their crops;
> - *Sustainability* – making sure that the environment is not harmed – recycling, reusing and replacing, and using alternative energy sources where possible;
> - *Food miles* – making the distance between food producer and shop as small as possible;
> - *Carbon footprint* – this is the measure of the impact of an activity on the environment; businesses can offset this through 'green' policies;
> - *Ethical investment* – investors may only want to invest in those businesses where they are assured that the business has a high standard of ethics.
>
> Energy use leaves a carbon footprint

Business aims and objectives

Have a go

Group activity

Look at the possible 'maximising' targets for businesses. Name a business that you think is aiming for each target. What can you say about the different kinds of business?

Discussion

Visit the websites of some top businesses and make a list of their mission statements. What similarities are there between them? Can you spot any current trends from this? Discuss what you think they have in common and what you think makes them different.

Web-based activity

Visit:
www.guardian.co.uk/environment/2007/may/17/rupertmurdoch.broadcasting
and read what Rupert Murdoch intends to do with the Sky media and publishing empire. Explain why you think he has set this target.

Quickfire questions

1. What is a business 'aim'?
2. What is a business 'objective'?
3. What is a 'mission statement'?
4. What does SMART stand for?
5. Outline why a business should always have SMART targets.
6. Name the three broad types of business objective.
7. List three things that a business might aim to maximise.
8. List three things that a business might aim to minimise.
9. List one objective of a small business that may not be appropriate for a larger business.
10. What is meant by 'social responsibility'?

Hit the spot

▸ Choose three businesses. Find out as much as you can about each business. Which do you think is the most successful? By what measure?

▸ Measure your own carbon footprint at **www.carbonfootprint.com** and then set your own aims and objectives so that you have your own environmental responsibility programme.

▸ Explain why businesses feel that it is necessary to set themselves targets. Which target do you think is the most important for a small business? Give reasons for your answer.

Cracking the code

Aim Long-term target.

Ethical Doing what is morally the right thing to do.

Labour turnover The number of people leaving and being replaced in a time period.

Mission statement A 'what we do and how we do it' long-term aim of a business.

Objective Shorter-term target, on the way to reaching an aim.

Social responsibility (often called corporate social responsibility or CSR) Environmental or social aims usually written into a CSR policy.

SECTION 2
STARTING A BUSINESS

Chapter 6
Stakeholders

IN THE NEWS

Coffee Nation

The founders of Coffee Nation were dissatisfied by the inconsistent quality of coffee found in the UK. They recognised that the high street coffee shops cropping up in towns around the country had created a taste for premium quality coffee amongst the consumer.

In 1999, Coffee Nation's founders set to work developing a self-service coffee machine concept that combined barista coffee, using fresh, quality ingredients, with the consistency, availability and ease of vending. This would eliminate the possibility for human error and allow retail, travel and leisure outlets to offer their customers great-tasting coffee.

Coffee Nation now has 60 employees. There are currently 650 sites where Coffee Nation drinks are sold. Each machine is connected to the internet and monitored by a dedicated helpline, so when machine faults are recorded, service engineers are on site within a matter of hours, whatever the time of day, to fix the problem.

Coffee Nation has a **policy** of fair trade and sources selected beans for its blend from Rainforest Alliance certified farms. This means the business will always pay a fair price for coffee beans and not use its buying strength to force down the price it has to pay, as well as supporting coffee farmers to preserve their natural eco-systems in their local area.

Persuading people to pay more to receive gourmet coffee has been cracked by Starbucks. Once people get used to drinking quality coffee, they are willing to return time and time again. Coffee Nation believes enough people will do this, even if this means paying a higher price for a much better quality product.

Coffee Nation's main challenge was to convince customers that good coffee can be obtained from a machine. Although some consumers are still resistant, Coffee Nation is successfully re-inventing its brand identity to engage consumers with the message that its coffee is made using fresh milk and real beans.

High-quality coffee 24 hours a day

Visit the Coffee Nation website at:
www.coffeenation.com

Stakeholders

> **Did you know…?**
>
> People often confuse the word 'stakeholder' with 'shareholder'. The words do look the same, after all! A shareholder is just one type of stakeholder, but there are many other stakeholders.

Stakeholder

A **stakeholder** is an individual or group of people that have an interest in a business. Stakeholders want the business to do well, because if it does, they benefit. Similarly, if the business fails, then stakeholders suffer in some way.

The main stakeholders are usually thought to be:

Employees

These are the people who work for a business in return for a wage or a salary. Quite often employees work for more than just money. A job might bring status and a sense of purpose to someone. If a business were to close, its employees would lose their incomes and have to look elsewhere for their livelihood. On the other hand, a successful business can afford to pay higher wages to its employees. A successful business could also afford to train employees to a higher standard. So, workers have an interest, or stake, in their employer doing well. This is particularly true when there is **unemployment** in the country. Someone who loses his or her job might find it very difficult to get another one.

Shareholders

A shareholder is someone who has bought a small part of a business. The shareholder will receive a share certificate for the money paid. In return, the shareholder will get a share of the profits that the business makes. This payment is usually called a **dividend**. A business that is doing well will be able to afford to pay a high dividend to its shareholders. If the business is making a loss, there will be no shareholders' dividend.

Customers

A successful business might be able to reduce the prices it charges customers. It will also be able to afford to buy better standard materials, or pay for better training for its employees. These would help to improve the quality of the products that customers buy. A failing business might try to cut corners with its product, reducing its quality.

An employee is a stakeholder

> **Did you know…**
>
> Some stakeholders are seen as more important than others. One business might see the customer as the most important stakeholder. Another business might just worry that its shareholders receive their dividends.

Once a business has closed down, of course, there will be less choice for customers.

Suppliers

When a business buys materials from a supplier it will usually receive credit. This means the business does not have to pay its bill straightaway. This allows the business time to make the money to pay the supplier. If the business is not successful, it might not be able to pay the supplier. Therefore, suppliers want the business to do well so they will get their bills paid! Coffee Nation takes its responsibility further than this. The business believes that it has a responsibility to pay a fair price for the coffee it uses. The business could buy coffee cheaper from other suppliers, but will only deal with responsible suppliers who ensure the growers receive a good income.

Creditors

Suppliers are a type of **creditor**, as the business owes them money. There are other types however. If a business has borrowed money from a bank, and most businesses do, the bank is a creditor.

The local community

This is a very general term that tends to cover the people within the area the business operates. Businesses have to pay taxes that are called rates to local councils. This money is used to provide services, such as street lighting and road maintenance in the area. If a business fails, the local council will no longer receive the rates from this business. There will be less money available for the council to spend on improving the **local community**.

Many businesses employ people who live in the area they operate. Wages paid to these employees will often be spent in local shops. This creates even more money for the local community.

Internal and external stakeholders

The different types of stakeholders can be seen as being internal or external Internal stakeholders are those directly connected with the business. These include employees and shareholders.

External stakeholders have an interest in the business, but are not actually part of the organisation. These would include suppliers, customers and the local community.

Everyone in the local area is a stakeholder

Stakeholders

Did you know…

Many businesses now like to state publicly who their stakeholders are. Business web pages will often have details of stakeholders. It's almost compulsory, it seems!

Summary

- Stakeholders are people who are affected by a business's success
- Stakeholders who are part of the business are said to be internal stakeholders
- Businesses have different views about which stakeholders are more important
- In the past, many businesses were only really been concerned about their owners, the shareholders

Core knowledge

When a business takes off, the person who starts it is probably going to be the person who also runs, or manages, it. The entrepreneur has put his or her money and time into the venture and obviously wants the business to do well. In most cases, 'doing well' means making a healthy profit.

Being successful, however, will not just depend on the owner and manager. There are other people that the business should not forget. Customers are important. Without customers, the business will not be able to sell its product or service and will soon be forced to close. A business that treats its customers badly will find it hard to keep them. Selling poor quality or even dangerous products will put customers off. They will probably go elsewhere next time. A plumber who regularly turned up late, for example, would get a poor reputation and find it harder to get business in the future.

Employees are another group the business should consider. In many businesses the employees are the people the customer deals with. If employees are not seen as being very important they will be unhappy working for the business. They will come across as not bothered, which will reflect badly on the business. Respecting employees is not just about paying them good wages. As with all humans, employees want to feel they belong and are doing a worthwhile job.

And more

Increasingly these days, businesses are taking a wider view of their stakeholders.

People are becoming more concerned about global warming and other environmental issues. Businesses need to be seen to be caring about these issues too, otherwise they could lose valuable customers. Many businesses have written statements or policies on what they will do to reduce their impact on the environment. So, the environment can also be seen as a stakeholder.

At one time, businesses didn't really think they had a commitment to the local community in which they operated. They provided jobs to local people and paid local taxes, and many thought that was all they needed to do.

Some people would argue that businesses are not genuinely concerned about issues such as the local community and environmental harm. Being environmentally friendly and caring for the local community costs money. If a business is not to lose out, then the extra money it receives from attracting additional customers with its caring image should be greater than the money it spends getting the caring image.

Business has an impact on the environment

Have a go!

Group activity

Working in a group, consider a business that believes that its most important stakeholders are:

- its employees, and
- the local community.

Describe what the business might do to look after these stakeholders. Are your suggestions free, or will they cost the business money? What will be the benefits to the business, if any?

Now, consider how the actions that you have described in your previous answer could affect these stakeholders:

- the owners of the business, and
- customers.

Discussion

These days, many businesses like to be seen to be supporting local charities. This was unusual 20 years ago. Does this mean that businesses are becoming more generous?

Stakeholders

Web-based activity

Go to the Coffee Nation web pages at **www.coffeenation.com**. Say which of the business's stakeholders are mentioned on the pages. Write a report stating what Coffee Nation is doing to help its stakeholders.

Quickfire questions

1. What is a stakeholder?
2. How are Coffee Nation's vending machines different from other vending machines?
3. List three of Coffee Nation's stakeholders.
4. How does Coffee Nation look after its customers?
5. What is a creditor?
6. Is an employee an internal or external stakeholder?
7. What is meant by fairtrade?
8. How might buying fairtrade coffee actually help Coffee Nation?
9. List three ways consumers would be affected if Coffee Nation were to go out of business.
10. Give three ways the local community might be affected when a business closes.

Hit the spot

- Give two reasons why a business might give money to a local school.
- Explain how the quality of a product or service can depend on how much interest the business takes in its employees
- Discuss whether shareholders are the more important than other stakeholders.

Cracking the code

Creditor A person or organisation that is owed money by a business. A bank that lends money becomes a creditor of the business.

Dividend The share of the profit a shareholder receives.

Local community The people and institutions that are associated with an area. There is often a sense of belonging.

Policy Rules or a set of guidelines used by a business.

Stakeholder Someone who has an interest in the success of a business.

Unemployment Those people who are seeking work, but unable to find suitable jobs are classed as unemployed. The government counts how many people are claiming job seekers' allowances to calculate the level of unemployment.

Chapter 7
Planning an enterprise

IN THE NEWS

Bigger Feet

While many of his friends were concerned about music and the latest fashions, Oliver Bridge found himself in front of BBC and CNN cameras. Oliver had just started a new business and the media were interested. What attracted them was that Oliver was a 15-year-old successful businessman. Oliver's success was no accident. The planning of his enterprise had been thought through carefully. He had taken advice and produced a detailed **business plan**.

Oliver understood that the media would be interested in his story and gaining **publicity** was an important part of his plan. After appearing on television, sales greatly improved.

Oliver's business, Bigger Feet, is an online shoe retailer for people who need much larger than average shoes. The business came about from Oliver's own frustration in trying to buy big enough shoes for his large feet. His complaints led to his mother suggesting that he started up his own business. The idea grew on him and he put together a plan.

After realising that several people at school also required large shoes, Bridge undertook some **market research**. He found that about a million people in the UK have large feet. Bigger Feet produce men's shoes from size 12 and ladies' shoes from size 9.

One problem Oliver did have was getting banks to lend him money. People under 18 cannot be sued for not repaying a loan. So banks require someone older to agree to pay if the young person defaults. Such a person is called a **guarantor**.

Oliver planned to do all the work, or to use willing family members to help. This way there was no need to employ staff, with the problems that can come with them. Oliver reasoned that if the business did take off, then he could hire any staff that he needed. Oliver's plan was to keep costs down as much as possible. His family house was used to provide a small office and storage space for the shoes. There was no need for expensive shops and staff.

Oliver said, 'A website allows you to put something across very professionally at a very low cost. Our website probably rivals a medium-sized business, when in fact we're working from a tiny office.' Oliver also found that when he goes on holiday, the internet gives him the flexibility to continue his business without interruption.

Oliver's research took him to trade shows in Europe to find out more about the market. He also managed to negotiate a deal with Leicestershire wholesaler, UK Distributors, to buy just the shoes he needed. This way he rarely has more than 30 to 40 pairs of shoes in his possession. Not buying in bulk meant that Bigger Shoes was not a credit risk to the wholesaler.

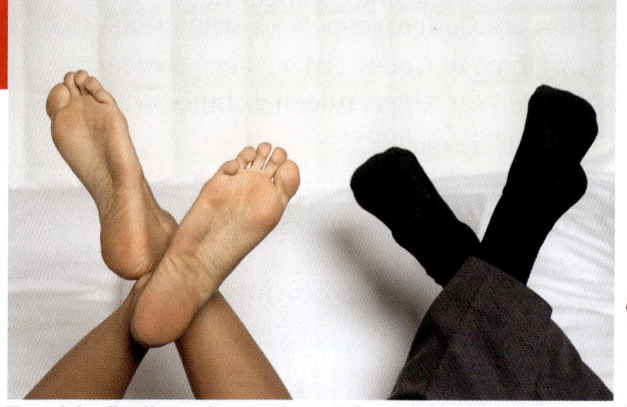

Trouble finding shoes that fit?

Planning an enterprise   41

> **Did you know...**
> Many businesses fail before they reach their second anniversary.

The business plan

Having a good business idea is not enough to make an entrepreneur successful. What needs to be done is to put the idea into practice. Before this can happen, the entrepreneur needs to check that the business will work. What equipment will be needed? What about employees? What is the market like? Where can materials be bought? All this needs careful planning.

One important resource is money. Unless the entrepreneur is fortunate enough to fund the project out of his or her own pocket, the money will have to be borrowed. Before banks give a loan, they will want to know that there is a good chance of the business being successful. Banks want to be reasonably confident that they will get their money back. The usual way to persuade banks to lend money is for the entrepreneur to produce a business plan.

Oliver's success in getting Bigger Feet started lay with his willingness to plan the business. A business plan is a document that outlines how the business will run during the first year or two. It should have enough detail, so any problems can be identified before it is too late. Some of the details are bound to be guesswork. It is impossible to say for sure, for example, whether people will like the product or service. It may be the best thing since sliced bread, or it could fall flat. The entrepreneur can only make a reasonable estimate of sales.

So, what is in a business plan? Business plans can be written in different ways, but most will contain this information each in its own section.

The business idea

What exactly is the product or service? How will it be different from what is already out there?

Management

Banks will want to be confident that the business will be well managed. If they have doubts about the managers they will be unwilling to put money into the venture. Details of the managers would include their business experience. Do the managers have a track record in the key areas of

> **Did you know...**
> Planned businesses have a much better chance of survival.

business, such as finance, marketing and managing employees?

The market

This section will probably include some information about who is likely to buy the product or service. Details on the competition and what makes this product different – its unique selling point.

Selling the product

How will the product be sold? Will it be sold through a retail outlet, like a shop or market stall, or through the internet?

Finances

This is the section that finds out if the idea is likely to be profitable and, if so, how long it will be before a profit is made. A key part of this section will be a forecast cash flow statement. This is a list of the money coming into and out of the business each month over the next year or so. All money needs to be there, including how much the owners of the business will be taking out for their own living expenses.

Summary

- A business plan is a document that tries to find out if an entrepreneur's idea is likely to be successful
- A business plan will usually include information about the product and its market, management, competition and cash flow
- Most investors will want evidence that a business has a good chance of success. They will usually ask to see the business plan.

Planning an enterprise

Core knowledge

A successful entrepreneur is not just someone who can come up with a great business idea. It is also a person who has the self-discipline to work out and check the details of the project before getting started, putting them down on paper. Only by doing this will the entrepreneur know that he or she has a business that can survive. The temptation might be to start up the idea before other entrepreneurs beat you to it and capture the market. Careful planning is important if you want to avoid losing a lot of money.

Very few businesses can be started for next to nothing. Start up costs have to be paid: advertisements even in local papers are expensive, the entrepreneur might need to buy a van, or other vehicle. Even a painter and decorator will spend hundreds, if not thousands, of pounds on ladders, a roof rack to carry the ladders, brushes, a storage place, and so on. Some of this money can be recovered if the business does not work out, but other costs will be lost.

There is also the entrepreneur's time to consider. Entrepreneurs are known for being hard working and prepared to put long hours into their business to help them become successful. If the business fails, then this time has been wasted and probably unrewarded.

Some entrepreneurs might write a business plan as a way of attracting investors or getting a loan from the bank. They may be tempted to exaggerate the details of the plan to make the project look better than it is. A careful investor will study the plan in detail and be worried about any aspect that looks unreasonable.

And more

A business plan is never an exact document. Much of it can best be described as educated guesswork. There will be things the entrepreneur will have a good idea about. The costs of materials can be negotiated from suppliers before the business starts. The entrepreneur will know the costs of advertising and how much an employee will cost. Some figures will be less reliable. An entrepreneur will have to 'speculate' how well the product will sell. Market research will provide some guidance on how well the product will be received by the market. But tastes change and there is no way of determining whether someone else has the same idea as you and is about to start a similar business.

All an entrepreneur can do in his or her business plan is to be honest, realistic and base as much on fact as possible.

AQA BUSINESS FOR GCSE: STARTING A BUSINESS

Have a go!

Activity

Come up with a possible business idea. Create a business plan to see if your idea has a chance of success.

Your teacher may even be able to invite a manager from a local bank to come into your school and give you feedback on your plan.

Quickfire questions

1. What is a business plan?
2. Who is likely to be interested in reading a business plan?
3. What are the main sections of a business plan?
4. Why do banks need guarantors?
5. What was different about Oliver Bridge's business?
6. What risks did Oliver take when starting his business?
7. Give two ways Oliver Bridge reduces the risks of failure.
8. Why would it be difficult for a new business to produce a cash flow forecast for the next three years?
9. Why do banks want to know about the previous management experience of an entrepreneur before giving him or her a loan?
10. What is meant by a credit risk?

Hit the spot

- Give three sections that a business plan is likely to have.
- Explain two things that a bank would look for within a business plan.
- Discuss whether a well-written business plan is more important that a good business idea.

Cracking the code

Business plan A detailed document that looks at the workings of a new business. It can be used to find out if the business has a chance of becoming successful.

Guarantor Someone who agrees to pay another person's debt.

Market research Finding out about competition and people's attitude towards a new product or service.

Publicity Using the media to raise people's interest in a product as a form of free advertising. Newspapers writing about a new film, and chat show hosts interviewing the film's stars, are examples of publicity.

Chapter 8
Types of business structure – unlimited liability

IN THE NEWS

Paula Vika Hair Designs

Paula Vika came to the UK from Angola in September 1999 with her six-year-old daughter. She was forced to leave the African state because of the civil war that was raging there. When she arrived in Britain she had nothing to her name. She recognised that if she was going to get on in her new country, she needed to learn how to speak English. So one of the first things she did was to enrol at a local college on an English-speaking course.

Paula was determined that she did not want to receive handouts, so set about finding a job for herself. At this point in her life, her only concern was to survive. She didn't expect to be running her own business within a short time. The **Job Centre** tried to place her in lots of different office jobs, but she couldn't get on because of her poor English. The Job Centre suggested that she should think about starting her own business. She looked into this but found it hard to get a loan from banks. She had no references and she was thought to be too great a risk to them.

She managed to find funding eventually from **The Prince's Trust**. Someone from the Trust interviewed her and offered her help writing a business plan. Paula had always styled friends' hair in Angola. Hairdressing seemed to be the obvious business route for her to take. Paula undertook some market research to see if the business had a chance of surviving. The Prince's Trust gave her a loan and her advisor suggested that she rent a chair at a local salon in Great Yarmouth. The Trust also pointed her in the direction of the **New Entrepreneur Scholarship**, where she could learn basic business skills.

Paula operated her own chair at somebody else's salon for 12 months. Her customers kept coming back asking for Paula to style their hair. She was always busy and she felt that it was now time to expand. Paula found a vacant salon in Norwich. She now employs two staff. One person works four days a week; the other works two. She also trains a young girl who comes in on Saturdays and school holidays.

Paula draws on her Angolan hairdressing experience in her salon. She offers a range of Afro-Portuguese contemporary and traditional styles. She is able to explain the services available to non-English speakers in five languages.

@ Visit Paula's website at:
www.paulavika.co.uk

> **Did you know…**
>
> Only about 50 per cent of small businesses are still trading after their first three years from initial set up.

What does unlimited liability mean for the entreprenuer?

Running your own business is not without risk. Getting a business off the ground requires money to buy equipment, materials and to pay wages. It can often be some time before the business is bringing in more money than it is costing the entrepreneur. The business will still have to pay its regular bills for items like rent, phones and electricity, even if it has not got many customers. An entrepreneur will often be allowed **credit** by suppliers. This means that when the business owner buys materials, the bill will not have to be paid for a month or two. So, it is quite possible for the business to build up large debts.

If the business idea was not as good as the entrepreneur first thought, the money coming in – the **revenue** – might dry up. Entrepreneurs in this position might find it increasingly difficult to pay their bills. The point may be reached when it is clear the business is never going to recover in the foreseeable future. The entrepreneur might decide at this point that it is no longer worth carrying on.

When this happens there is still the problem of unpaid bills. The debts owed to the business's **creditors** still have to be paid. The owner of the business is liable for the debts that he or she has built up. The owner is said to have unlimited liability. This means that even if the business fails, the owner has to settle the bills. The laws on unlimited liability are very old. They lay down rules on what personal possessions the owner must sell to get the money needed to pay off creditors.

Bankruptcy

If an entrepreneur is not paying his or her bills, creditors might even decide to go to court to have the entrepreneur declared **bankrupt**. This only happens when they feel there is no chance that the business will recover. Creditors are unlikely to get all of their money back if this happens. They know, however, that it will stop things getting worse. Once an entrepreneur is declared bankrupt by court, the business will probably stop trading and any possessions – or **assets** – will be sold.

> **Did you know…**
>
> Business failure is seen differently in different countries. In the UK it is still seen as a personal failure. In other countries, such as the USA, it is viewed as a learning opportunity.

Types of business structure – unlimited liability

In some cases, an unsuccessful entrepreneur can even make himself/herself bankrupt. This is known as voluntary bankruptcy.

Someone who has been declared bankrupt will be freed from most of his or her debts. The bankrupt person will be banned from running another business for a number of years, but will then have the opportunity to have a fresh start.

Did you know...

Richard Branson had two failed businesses before he was 15 years old. Yet he went on to become a highly successful billionaire entrepreneur.

Summary

- Having a good business idea is no guarantee that the business will be successful
- Most small businesses have unlimited liability, which means the owners are responsible for all the debts they build up
- Unlimited liability means the owner of the business still needs to pay outstanding bills, even if the business closes down
- If a person is declared bankrupt, he or she is no longer responsible for debts

Core knowledge

Some people believe that anyone who runs a business must be rich. This is far from the truth. Everyone who starts a business runs a risk. If the business fails the owner still has to pay off the debts that have built up. If things go wrong, a business idea could be very costly. This is what puts many people off starting their own business.

There are ways an entrepreneur can avoid losing a great deal of money. In fact, a good entrepreneur will not rush into business without trying to reduce the chances of failure and bankruptcy.

Finding out if customers will actually buy the entrepreneur's product rather than that of a competitor is important. This process is known as market research and will be studied in a later chapter.

There are other things can be done to minimise risk. Starting small and expanding when the idea has proved it can work makes sense. This is advice that Paula Vika followed. Rather than opening up her own salon straightaway, Paula rented a chair in another salon. Only when she was sure she had a good chance of success did she look for her own salon.

And more

Having unlimited liability can put people off starting a business. Many will consider the benefits of becoming a limited company very attractive and complete the necessary paperwork to achieve this. The process is discussed in the next chapter.

Another way for an entrepreneur to minimise risk is to lease equipment. Leasing simply means renting, rather than buying outright. The entrepreneur doesn't actually own this equipment but if things do not work out, it can be sent back to the leaser. There won't be any loan repayment to worry about if the business fails. There are other advantages of leasing. The equipment can be exchanged when more up-to-date equipment becomes available. Often this newer equipment will be no more expensive to lease. In addition, the lease contract will probably include maintenance and repairing faults. This means the entrepreneur can plan a budget without having to worry about repair or replacement bills.

Essential equipment for business may be bought or leased

Keeping the number of employees to a minimum is another strategy. Employees have to be paid even if there is very little business coming in. There are also laws giving redundancy payments to unneeded employees when they have to leave. This will probably mean the owner having to work long hours, but the risks are reduced.

Have a go!

Activity: Bankruptcy

Find out what the laws on bankruptcy are. Produce an information leaflet or poster containing this information. Imagine someone thinking of starting a new business will read the poster/leaflet. Try not to put the person off starting up, but make sure it contains a clear outline of the law.

You will find the information on the internet. www.insolvency.gov.uk and www.insolvencyhelpline.co.uk/bankruptcy are just two sites.

Types of business structure – unlimited liability

Quickfire questions

1. What is meant by unlimited liability?
2. Give two ways an entrepreneur might lose money when a business fails.
3. How did Paula Vika create a unique selling point for her business?
4. Why are banks often reluctant to lend money to new businesses?
5. What is voluntary bankruptcy?
6. What is leasing?
7. Outline how leasing works.
8. Explain why creditors may not want to declare a poor payer bankrupt.
9. Why might an entrepreneur still find it difficult to pay bills even if the business is selling many goods?
10. Does bankruptcy mean an entrepreneur has failed?

Hit the spot

- Describe two reasons why a new business might not make as much revenue as the entrepreneur expected it to make.
- Explain two ways Paula Vika helped reduce the chances of failing in business.
- Discuss whether the risks of starting a business are greater than the possible rewards.

Cracking the code

Assets Property or possessions owned by an entrepreneur or a business.

Bankrupt An entrepreneur who is unable to pay his/her bills. Receivers will take control of the business and sell off its assets. Creditors may then receive some of the money the business owes them.

Credit Buying goods or services and paying after they have been received.

Creditor Someone to whom a business owes money.

Job Centre A government-funded organisation that tries to find suitable work for job seekers.

New Entrepreneur Scholarship An organisation that helps people from disadvantaged backgrounds and areas to get started in business.

The Prince's Trust A charity started by the Prince of Wales that provides funding and support to unemployed young people who want to start their own businesses.

Revenue The money coming in from the sale of goods. This is sometimes called turnover.

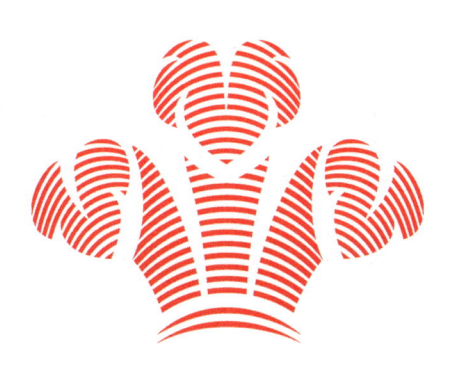

Prince's Trust

Chapter 9
Limited liability companies

IN THE NEWS

Innocent Smoothies

innocent

A spectacular success

Three young university friends started Innocent in 1999. None of them had any experience in drink manufacturing, nor did they have any financial backing. Despite these things Innocent's success has been spectacular.

Innocent's three founders, Richard Reed, Adam Balon and Jon Wright, had wanted to run a business together since their days at university. When they graduated they went their separate ways into jobs in business. But they still held on to their dream and it was always the main topic of conversation whenever they met.

The idea for Innocent Drinks came from looking at their own hectic urban lifestyles. As busy professionals they were working long hours, not finding the time to visit the gym and relying on fast food. After considering many possible products, the entrepreneurs came up with the idea of selling fruit smoothies.

They knew that people were becoming more health conscious, but they were not sure that people would be prepared to pay £2 for a 250ml drink. To find out if the idea would work, in 1999 they took their drinks to a jazz festival. By their stall they had a sign that asked the question: Do you think we should give up our jobs to make smoothies? Customers were asked to place their empty cups in one of two bins: Yes or No. There were far more cups in the Yes bin, so they took the plunge and resigned from their jobs.

As they had absolutely no experience in fruit or the drinks market, going from idea to reality obviously involved doing some research. 'We went away and just kept buying fruit and making up recipes that we thought tasted good,' recalls Reed. 'Then, once we had these drinks that we liked and our friends liked, we just needed to know if other people would go for it.'

However, the move to self-employment wasn't, well, a smooth one. One of the key obstacles was securing finance. Not only did they have a relatively expensive product with a short shelf life and no experience in the sector, it seemed they were in the wrong place at the wrong time. The three entrepreneurs were unable to pay themselves salaries at first. Times were very tight: their overdraft was getting bigger and bigger and they ended up having to pay their bills using their credit cards.

In the end, Innocent secured the funding it needed from a **business angel** but there were still obstacles to overcome. As a limited company, the investor knew that at worst, he would only lose as much

The moment of choice

money as he had invested into Innocent. He would not have to sell his personal possessions to pay any outstanding debts if Innocent failed.

Five years on and 10 million sales later, Innocent drinks are in shops across the country and word is spreading. But despite the overwhelming growth, until last summer Innocent hadn't spent a penny on advertising.

Innocent also gives away drinks to the homeless, plants trees, encourages recycling and donates to the third world, while its entire staff are treated to a snow boarding trip every year, awarded £2000 for the birth of each child and invited to apply for a £1000 scholarship to achieve something they've always wanted to do. 'Like recording a single or going surfing,' explains Reid.

The three founders gave up their jobs in 1999 and Innocent became a limited company in June 2000.

Check out Innocent's website at: www.innocentdrinks.co.uk

Did you know...

The multinational Virgin Group is a private limited company. Its main owner, Richard Branson, turned the business into a public limited company is 1984. However, Branson was so dissatisfied with public investors that he brought Virgin back to a private limited company two years later.

Limiting liability

A small business will always remain small unless the owner can raise capital to expand. A retailer, for example, might expand by buying or renting new shops. Alternatively, the retailer could buy out another business and increase in size this way. However it is done, it will need money. Probably this will be more money than the original business is able to provide from its trading.

Entrepreneurs will try to persuade others to put in **capital**, in return for a share of any future profits the business might make. These **shareholders** will often have very little to do with the running of the business. They have to trust that the managers are controlling things in a way that keeps their investment safe and gives them a decent dividend. Shareholders do not want to find that the company is losing money or, worse still, they are liable for debts of the company. After all, it is not because of them that the business is going under.

Clearly, shareholders would be reluctant to lend money if the risks are too high. They would not want to lose their house and car because managers were not running the business properly. For this reason, a law was passed many years ago that restricted just how much a shareholder could lose. If a business is found to be operating in a sound way, the shareholders could be granted limited liability status. This means that the most the owners of the business, the shareholders, could lose is the money they used to buy their shares. They will not be called upon to sell their personal possessions to pay the business's debts.

Creating a private limited company

A business goes through a process called **incorporation** in order to gain limited liability status. This involves giving information to the authorities, proving the business is operating properly and is secure. A business can be identified as a limited company by the abbreviation Ltd after its name. Another type of limited company is a public limited company, plc, which will be looked at in another book.

A private limited company must show that it has limited liability. This is usually done by putting Ltd after its name, which is an abbreviation for limited. This warns suppliers that they might not receive all of their money if the business fails. There are restrictions on who can buy shares in the company. The shares cannot be sold to the general public. It is often just immediate family who have shares, or people who work in the business.

A sign of limited liability

Summary

- The owners of a business with unlimited liability are responsible for all of its debts. The owners may be required to sell their own personal possessions to pay off **creditors**.
- If the business goes through the process of incorporation it can be granted limited liability status. This means the owners, the shareholders, can only lose the money they put into the business. They are not required to sell their personal possessions to pay the company's debts if the business fails.
- Private limited companies cannot sell shares to the general public

Core knowledge

If somebody asked you to put money into his or her business, you would expect to have a say in how the business was being run – it is your money you are investing, after all! You may, however, have neither the time nor the expertise to monitor the business closely. You have to trust the entrepreneur is running the business properly, so your money is safe.

So what happens if the business does not do well? You took a risk when you lent the money, so you should be prepared to accept you might lose some, or all of it. What you wouldn't want is to find that not only have you lost all the money you put into the business, but you are also expected to sell off your house to pay the business's debts. This is what could happen with a business with unlimited liability. The owners, which include you, would have to sell their personal possessions to pay the creditors.

If you put money into a limited business, however, you would only lose up to the value of your investment. There would be no need to sell your own personal assets to settle the debts of the business. Limited liability was introduced to protect investors from losing their own property, even though they were not responsible for the failure of the business.

Limited companies will have one or more directors who look after the shareholders' interests.

Limited liability companies

And more

It is for this reason that many businesses choose to become 'incorporated', particularly if they are expanding. It is not a particularly difficult or an expensive process, but it does make it easier for a business to attract investors. People will be more inclined to put money into a business if they know the size of the risk, or their liability, that they are taking.

Incorporation means that a business is given a separate legal status from its owners. A limited business can be sued in its own right, rather than the owner taken to court, if something goes wrong. The business can also sue others, such as someone who owes it money, but is reluctant to pay. Property can also be held in the business's name.

To become a limited business, two documents have to be written. These are the Memorandum of Association and the Articles of Association. The first document, the Memorandum, just describes the business, giving basic details: its address, names of shareholders, and so on. The Articles document contains more information. It includes how decisions will be made in the business: details about the regular meeting with shareholders – the AGM – and how profits will be shared.

Unlike an unlimited business that can keep its financial affairs to itself, a limited company must send its accounts to Companies House. These can then be seen by anyone who is interested, including competitors. It is for this reason that some unlimited businesses prefer to remain unlimited.

Have a go!

Web-based activities

Go on the internet and find local businesses that have limited liability. Mark on a map of the area in which you live where these businesses are located.

Use the internet to research more about Innocent Smoothies. Produce an information sheet about the company's involvement in good causes. The sheet should be written for young readers and contain suitable illustrations.

AQA BUSINESS FOR GCSE: STARTING A BUSINESS

Quickfire questions

1. What is a creditor?
2. What does the abbreviation Ltd stand for?
3. What is a shareholder?
4. Why would investors be more willing to put money into a limited company?
5. What do we mean by a business angel?
6. How did the three men who started Innocent find out whether the idea of selling smoothies was likely to succeed?
7. What is the role of a director?
8. Why might a business find it difficult to expand without limited liability status?
9. Why might a business not want its financial accounts to be available to the general public?
10. Why might a member of the public be reluctant to buy shares in a private limited company?

Hit the spot

- Describe two benefits the owners of Innocent Ltd had when they gained limited liability status.
- Explain why a supplier would want to know if a business that had placed an order was a limited company.
- Discuss: If limited liability is such a good thing, why do not all businesses become limited companies?

Cracking the code

Business angel A private investor who is willing to put money into a new business, where a bank would probably not take the risk.

Capital The value of the funds put into a business. Capital is what is used to buy the equipment the business needs to operate.

Creditor Someone to whom a business owes money. This could be a supplier or even an employee who is paid a week or month in arrears.

Shareholder A person who owns a share of a business.

Chapter 10
Business location decisions

IN THE NEWS

Style Gardens Limited

Welsh entrepreneurs, brothers Graham and Ian Pugh and Carl Hitchings, planned to open a garden centre and were looking for a suitable location. Pugh was already an established name in the garden centre business. The brothers' grandfather opened a small nursery in Rhiwbina, Cardiff in the 1930s. Their father Colin established a garden centre at Cardiff in 1968 followed by a nursery and growing centre at Caerphilly. So the entrepreneurs knew the importance of location when it came to deciding where to site their enterprise.

The site of old, but rundown, nurseries at Wenvoe on the main gateway to the Vale of Glamorgan road was eventually chosen. There was enough space for future expansion on the 7-acre site. The A4050 road which bordered the site is one of the busiest roads in Wales. The Wenvoe location was attractive, being on the main route to and from Barry, the Vale and Cardiff Airport. It was conveniently placed for attracting **passing trade**, and just a few minutes' drive from Cardiff.

Despite the site having housed a nursery before, much had to be done to update it to attract customers. Their new company, Style Gardens, started a £1 million transformation of the site. This involved clearing the land, erecting new buildings and extensive landscaping works, including a new frontage on to the Port Road. It was no good having a good location if the garden centre did not look attractive and inviting to customers.

The company now employs 25 full- and part-time staff – most of whom were taken on in the past two years to keep pace with expansion. It plans to double its workforce and the whole site's current £3.5 million turnover within five years.

@ Take a look at the Style Gardens website at:
www.stylegardens.co.uk

> **Did you know…**
>
> Most entrepreneurs start their businesses in the area in which they live.

Locating a business

One of the most important decisions that an entrepreneur has to make is where his or her business is to be based. Many entrepreneurs will choose to run their businesses from their own homes, in order to keep costs down. Others might recognise that to get the best chances of success, it may be necessary to move somewhere else. This might even mean moving to a different part of the country, or abroad.

The growth of internet shopping has reduced the importance of location for many businesses. The internet has allowed even the smallest business to access a global market. Items can be bought by customers using the internet and then delivered to them using a courier or the postal service. Of course, the internet would not be suitable if a personal service, such as hairdressing or plumbing, was being offered. It would also be difficult if the products being sold were very fragile or perishable.

Running a business at home

There are several factors that a new business might need to take into account when the owner decides where to locate his or her business.

The owners of Style Gardens Limited took care to ensure that they chose the right location for their new business venture. South Wales was somewhere they were familiar with and family members had been successful in setting up similar businesses in the area. The Wenvoe site was big enough to allow for future expansion without moving to larger **premises**. Wenvoe was also close to the large population of Cardiff.

The market

Some businesses have to be located close to their markets. This could be because the product they sell costs a lot to transport. Having a nearby market is important to service providers, such as shops. Customers would not travel vast distances just to go to one particular supermarket, if there were others much closer. Also, a plumber who lived 30 miles from his main market would spend a long time each day travelling.

Road system

A good road system, or infrastructure, allows a business to be located further afield. Time can be saved if a business is located close to a major road or a motorway. Goods can be transported more quickly and customers can reach the business without a difficult journey. It is for this reason that many industrial estates and shopping malls are located near to good road systems.

Available employees

Businesses need employees, so there needs to be suitable people living locally. If the business needs employees with particular skills, local people should have these skills, or they will need

Business location decisions

to be trained. If low-skilled workers are needed, a suitable number should live within easy reach of the business. Low-skilled workers are less likely to own a car, so they will need a place of work on a bus route, or within walking distance.

Competition

Having a lot of similar businesses in an area often seems a bad thing for a business. Competition tends to bring prices down as one business tries to attract customers from another. Even so, an entrepreneur might still want to move into a location where there are several other similar businesses. The product or service being offered must be popular to attract several businesses. It is possible that one more business could survive in the market.

Many businesses rely on a good road system

Did you know...

Local councils sometimes provide small industrial buildings for entrepreneurs to use at low rents. The councils realise that bringing businesses into the area will lower unemployment and create more wealth in the area.

Summary

- The location of a business is important and can make the difference between success and failure
- There are many things that businesses need to take into account to work out which is the best location. These include: how close customers live, how easy it is to get goods in and out, the level of competition in the area and whether suitable employees can be obtained.
- The internet has transformed where businesses are located. Any business can produce a web page that can be used to attract customers and gain orders. Buying goods through the internet is becoming increasingly popular.
- For some entrepreneurs it is more important to operate close to where they live than move to where the business might be more profitable

Core knowledge

Many new businesses will operate close to where the entrepreneur lives. The business may actually be based in the owner's house. A builder may, for example, use a room in his or her own house as an office, and possibly own a yard where the building materials are stored. Work may be undertaken within, let's say, a 20-mile radius of one of these places. Any more and too much time could be spent travelling to the site each day. The range in which our builder can operate will depend on how good the roads are in the area. A motorway system might make it realistic to travel much further to a job.

If there were a lot of competition for builders in a particular area, a new builder might find it more profitable to move to a new town where there is less competition. Too many competitors means the business will have to look harder for work and accept a lower price for the job. Having a **USP** (a unique selling point) might help to attract customers.

If the product is expensive to buy with a target market of wealthy consumers, such as the expensive coffee vending machines produced by Coffee Nation (in Chapter 6), it will need to be placed in a suitable location. It would be no good having an expensive coffee vending machine at a day centre for the unemployed.

And more

Some businesses are more mobile than others. By that we mean they find it easier to move to and operate in other locations. If a business is selling a product that can be delivered by post or courier, then the actual location of the factory or storage facility is not that important. Orders can be parcelled and sent off from a nearby post office each day, or collected by a courier service. Such a business will probably choose to be located where the costs are cheapest.

Service providers, on the other hand, need to be close to the market. It would be difficult to operate a hairdressing salon, for example, in an industrial estate on the edge of a town. It will need to be in the high street where it would be seen by potential customers. Few people would like to travel a long way to have their hair cut.

There is a theory that businesses will tend to be located where they can make the most profit. Not everyone believes that is true though. Many entrepreneurs would not be prepared, for instance, to move to the other side of the country. They might prefer to remain close to where they were brought up, even if this means that their costs are higher and there is more competition. Also, established businesses cannot easily uproot and go somewhere else that would be more profitable. This is sometimes called **industrial inertia**.

Business location decisions

Have a go!

Group activity

If possible visit an industrial estate. If a visit is difficult then a virtual visit can take place by going to a website, such as **www.manor-industrial-estate.co.uk** or **www.youngsindustrialestate.co.uk**

Study the industrial estate and produce a report identifying:

- The type of businesses located there;
- Where the likely markets for the products are;
- What the communication systems are like – such as roads, motorways, railway stations and airports.

Find a map on the internet of the area in which Style Gardens is located. The postcode is CF5 6AD. On this map clearly mark the reasons that makes the location suitable for a garden centre.

Quickfire questions

1. What is a garden centre?
2. What is an industrial estate?
3. What is meant by a market?
4. What is a courier?
5. Why do many entrepreneurs prefer to run their businesses from their own homes?
6. Explain why prices tend to be cheaper when there are several businesses in an area selling the same good or service.
7. How does the closeness of Cardiff help Style Gardens?
8. Why are some people still reluctant to buy goods on the internet?
9. Describe how businesses might benefit from being close to an airport.
10. Explain why many industrial estates are found on the outskirts of towns, rather than the centre of them.

Hit the spot

- Give two reasons why a business might want to set up in an area with many competitors.
- Explain how a good motorway system can make it cheaper for a business to operate.
- Discuss whether it is a good idea to locate a business in an area where there is high unemployment.

Cracking the code

Industrial inertia A term used when a business remains in a location when the reasons why it started there no longer exist.

Passing trade Custom that comes from people who happen to notice the business when they are in the area.

Premises The buildings and land belonging to a business.

USP Unique Selling Point, the things that make one business stand out from its competitors.

SECTION 3

MARKETING

Chapter 11
Researching the market

IN THE NEWS

V2Go

Entrepreneurs Stephen Marsden and James Whittaker spotted a gap in the market when they tried to find a vegetarian or vegan fast-food outlet in their local town centre. Surrounded by burger bars, meat pizzas and fried chicken outlets, they decided that there was a place for a vegetarian-based outlet. They tried looking for similar outlets, but their research revealed that the competition was not particularly strong and, in some cases, there was no competition at all. For instance, in the Trafford Centre in Manchester, there were no vegetarian options. This, then, was a good place to put the first of what they hoped would be many branches. They contacted the Vegetarian Society, which was happy to back the project.

V2Go was established as the first real vegetarian fast-food operation to open in a shopping centre in the UK. Whittaker is quoted as saying: 'We were acutely aware of the lack of choice available to veggie consumers and for those seeking a healthier meal option. Although most fast-food outlets have a vegetarian option the choice is somewhat limited. We want to provide delicious and wholesome meals and snacks which as well as being vegetarian are healthy. We believe we've now got a product range which will appeal to most tastes. We will also be introducing low fat symbols for the calorie aware consumer.' After securing the success of the first branch, they looked at expanding. 'Our ultimate aim,' he said, 'is to have a V2Go in every city of the UK.' Market research has also shown that the business has to cater for a range of tastes. Research has shown that V2Go has broad appeal with non-vegetarians as well as veggie customers. In an interview in the *Manchester Evening News*, James said: 'Many of our customers are vegetarian though we know from research up to 40 per cent are what we call "fair weather veggies" who succumb to the odd bacon sandwich now and then but, for whatever reason, are fussy about eating meat and enjoy soya or Quorn-based foods. Up to 80 per cent of our customers are women who are both calorie and health conscious and love the fact they can enjoy fast food without high fat content.' V2Go has now expanded, become a private limited company, and gone international with an outlet in Belfast.

Source: Trafford Centre Publicity Material; *Manchester Evening News*

V2Go set up its first branch at Manchester's Trafford Centre

@ The Vegetarian Society can be found at **www.vegsoc.org**. What help do you think organisations such as this can give to particular businesses?
Read the article, published in *The Independent* newspaper, at **www.independent.co.uk/life-style/food-and-drink/features/fast-food-neednt-be-junk-food-523835.html**. If you were setting up a food business, what information from this would be useful to you?

Researching the market

> **Did you know...**
> You should always try to use appropriate methods to display the information. Before using a graph or chart, for example, think about whether it will make the data clearer or not. Using the right graph to display certain information is one way of making sure that your message is clear.

Market research

Purpose

The purpose of market research is to find out if a product, or idea, is viable in a market. It is important that the business does not confuse promotion with research. Research requires feedback – in other words, there must be a response in terms of data collected. Handing out flyers or putting up posters is promotion, not market research. Both sides of a market need researching.

- *Looking at demand*: if there is high demand for a good or service, it is likely that there are already many competitors. If research shows good levels of demand, and few competitors, then there is a gap in the market.

- *Looking at supply*: if there are few or no competitors in a market, this could mean that there is a **gap in the market**. Equally, it could mean that there is little demand. It could also mean that the existing businesses are able to stop others from entering the market. Maybe they have all the supply tied up? Or are able to keep customers loyal?

Methods

A small business is limited in the market research it can carry out. It would be pointless (and expensive) for example, to conduct a survey in several cities. To find out about the supply side, the business could use local telephone and business directories to see if competition existed. It could also obtain information from its suppliers (a supplier survey), to find out who else they supplied, and whether any of these were local and likely to be competitors. It could also use internet search engines. If competitors are found, this does not mean that there is no room for the business and a visit to a competitor (as a customer) could give good information about the best way to compete.

To find out if there is any demand is harder. This is because, to be accurate, the research needs to target the right customers. One method could be to telephone a selection of customers (a telephone survey), but there would need to be help in identifying who to telephone. V2Go, for instance, could have contacted members of the Vegetarian Society in Manchester. Other methods could include door-to-door surveys and approaching people on the street or in the shopping centre where they intended to put the business.

New technology

Small businesses have the problem of a limited budget for research, and a difficulty in targeting it effectively. New technology can be a great help in collecting information and keeping down costs. Professional market research information is available on the internet, but is costly to collect and present, so tends to be expensive. The small business can, however, carry out competitor surveys using internet search engines. It can also, for free, visit the websites of competitors to

> **Did you know...**
> Businesses may collect data themselves or use a specialist agency. Even small businesses can benefit from the services of an agency if they choose carefully.

AQA BUSINESS FOR GCSE: SETTING UP A BUSINESS

Primary research: a door-to-door survey

to give feedback – these are extensively used in hotels and other service industries. V2Go could ask, for instance, what else customers would like to see on the menu. By collecting customers' email addresses, the business can carry out email surveys at a fraction of the cost of a postal survey.

compare prices, product ranges, special offers, etc. Research will be much more accurate if competitor websites are actually visited. The business can then see exactly what is offered, how it is priced, and judge levels of customer service.

Primary research: asking for customer feedback

Continuing research

Market research does not stop once the business is established. It helps the business to decide not only what to sell, but also what direction its products should take. What changes or developments would attract customers and/or help the business to compete more effectively? Comment sheets could be issued for customers

Did you know...

There is a difference between data and information. Data is raw facts, figures, statistics, etc. Information is when this data has been turned into a form that can be easily understood.

Summary

- Market research is used to find out if a product will sell
- Market research needs to look at possible demand and at competition
- Research may be either primary (first-hand) or secondary (already published)
- Small businesses can carry out only limited market research
- Some research information, such as directories, is freely available
- New technology can help small businesses to find out about competition
- Research needs to be ongoing, to check if customer demand or competition is changing

Researching the market

Core knowledge

Primary research (also called 'field' research) is data that has not been collected before. It is 'first-hand' information. Primary research may be expensive, but it can be targeted to collect exactly the information needed. Methods include:

- Questionnaires and surveys carried out among customers (or potential customers) and suppliers – there is a whole science to asking both the right question and the right type of question so that responses can be sufficiently easy to analyse, or sufficiently detailed to provide the information being sought.
- Observation – traffic counts, footfall counts, watching customer behaviour.
- Interviews – either face to face or via telephone (face to face is more effective but more expensive).
- Focus groups – small groups of people who are asked in-depth questions to measure their reactions to products; a new advertisement may, for example, be shown first to a focus group so that they can react and comment on it; a new product may be 'tasted and tested' by such a group.
- Electronic information – usually only available to large businesses, such as till roll and loyalty card information (e.g. who bought what, when; who came back; how often?).

Secondary research is research that has been previously published. There are very good sources of secondary data such as government figures and statistics and numerous less reliable sources. The problem with secondary research is that, while some of it may be cheap (it may even be free – government collected statistics are available at www.statistics.gov.uk) much of it may not be exactly what the business wants. Often secondary research may only provide background information. For example, secondary data may provide evidence of a demand trend in the direction of healthy living. It would need the focused primary research of a business to be able to see if it could take advantage of such a trend.

Primary research: a survey of passers-by

AQA BUSINESS FOR GCSE: SETTING UP A BUSINESS

And more

Research can also look at what potential customers may or may not be prepared to pay for. A **customer analysis** is useful in this respect. A business needs to have a good idea of its 'ideal customer' and may be able to draw up a picture of 'the person' that they want to attract. To whom is the product or service going to appeal? This is called 'customer profiling' and is used to help target customers. Example questions that could help to build a customer profile are:

- what age should the customer be?
- what income group?
- what interests and hobbies should they have?
- what level of education will they have reached?
- where do we expect them to live?
- do they have access to the internet?
- what sort of added value will they respond to?

Often such research is disguised as something else – many competition entries ask for basic information about the entrant while warranties and guarantees will often only be validated by the purchaser filling in details on a guarantee card.

The data collected may be, as with all research, either quantitative or qualitative. Quantitative data consist of figures, graphs, tables and statistics. Usually, the bigger the sample, the more accurate the data, but this tends to make collecting such data expensive. National data is collected by the Office of National Statistics and published on the web. Qualitative data consists of opinions and views. It is unlikely to be statistically accurate but will help to give a complete picture. In some cases, qualitative data (the opinions of local residents, for example) may be more powerful than quantitative.

Have a go

Group activity

Decide on a new product or idea for which you think there will be a demand. Draw up a mini-questionnaire for use in your group. Ask just ten questions. Try out the questionnaire on your group and draw up the answers. You should then, between you, decide two things:

1. Were the questions correctly phrased and did they give useful information?
2. Is there demand for the product that you have suggested?

Discussion

Draw up a map of your local village centre or shopping centre. Shade in the different types of business, e.g. hairdressers, newsagents, estate agents, different types of retail outlet. Decide what you think is missing from the area and would therefore be a good business to set up. Try to convince the other members of your class or group that this is a good business idea for the area by collecting appropriate evidence.

Researching the market

Web-based activity

Reviews of V2Go in Manchester (and other restaurants) can be read at **www.veggieheaven.com/uk/england/manchester/29/V2GO/**. How helpful do you think such review sites are to the business, to other customers, to competitors? Would such reviews form part of market research?

Quickfire questions

1. What is the purpose of market research?
2. What are the two general areas that should be researched?
3. Suggest three ways for a small business to carry out research.
4. What could a business research using the internet?
5. Name one problem that small businesses have with market research.
6. Give two circumstances where a business should carry out market research.
7. What is meant by 'primary' research?
8. Give three examples of primary research methods.
9. What is meant by 'secondary' research?
10. Give one example of secondary market research information that is free.

Hit the spot

- Describe the two main areas where market research should be carried out.
- Explain the difference between data and information.
- Which do you think is more effective, primary or secondary research? Explain the reasons that you think so.

Cracking the code

Customer analysis Building a picture of the 'ideal' customer from customer behaviour.

Gap in the market Where demand exists in a market but there is no product to fulfil it.

Primary research Field research; research that has not been carried out before.

Questionnaires A list of questions used for primary information.

Secondary research Desk research; research that has been previously carried out or published for another body or purpose.

Chapter 12
Marketing mix elements and price

IN THE NEWS

Despite recent problems in the air industry as a whole, easyJet and Ryanair continue to make a profit on the back of their low price model of air transport. easyJet has been in operation since 1995 and in 2007 made over £200 million profit carrying over 37 million passengers. As consumer demand for low cost travel has increased, both airlines have expanded. Ryanair, which started in 1997, is Europe's biggest low price carrier and the third largest airline in Europe measured by passenger numbers. Measured in terms of international passenger numbers, it is the largest airline in the world.

Costs – and prices – are kept low through quick turn round times for planes and by cutting out 'frills' and 'extras' such as complimentary food and drink. Charges are also made for many of the services that air travellers might take for granted, such as baggage carrying and check-in. The marketing mix for these carriers also includes a different product, in that they fly direct from city to city (or to outlying airports of cities) rather than using a 'hub and spoke' system. Many airlines carry passengers on what may be loss-making short services to their 'hub' airport, from which they then fly to long haul international destinations. For instance, Heathrow is British Airways' major hub, Amsterdam Schiphol is KLM's and Chicago that of United Airlines.

Both carriers have also been quick to see the cost-saving benefits of new technology, such as internet booking, with easyJet being the first to introduce web booking (in 1998) and then to abandon any other form of booking. Ryanair's website was introduced in 2000. By 2001 it was taking 75 per cent of all bookings and, like easyJet's, now takes all bookings. Ryanair has also been at the forefront of promotion offering, in 2007, 1 million seats at 1 penny each.

Other changes have squeezed airlines in general. While the low cost, low price model is still succeeding, but at a much slower pace, other models have gone out of business. Silverjet decided on a very different marketing mix – a luxury product and high price, promoted to business travellers. It established as a business-class only airline in 2004, flying to Dubai and New York, but went out of business in 2008, hit by the fall in demand for air transport that was causing all the airlines to look again at their business model and current marketing mix.

'No frills' air travel has been very successful

@ Airlines don't have to be huge but can be quite small businesses. Do a search to see what you can find out about Danny Reilly, who set up an airline – Nexus – when he was just 18.
easyJet and Ryanair each have their own websites where you can find information about the businesses.

> **Did you know...**
>
> Airlines can also be pretty small businesses, offering a particular service as a product, at a particular price and to a limited market. Palmair is based on a single route – but also on a particular price structure. It operates a single aircraft from Bournemouth and has twice been voted (in *Holiday Which* magazine) the top-rated UK airline.

Marketing mix

The **marketing mix** is the term given to the way that an entrepreneur sells a product. It is the mixture, or balance, of the various elements that go into making a sale. A successful business depends on its product being offered to customers at the right price, in the right place and with appropriate and effective promotion methods. This is often called 'the Four Ps' – product, price, promotion and place. Different businesses will adopt different mixes – some leading on product, some (like the low-price airlines above) leading on price. Some will rely heavily on advertising, while some will rely on reputation and 'word-of-mouth'. For others, it is the convenience of distribution that is the most important factor (such as banking services made available 24/7 over the internet). Most small businesses will have a limited budget for their marketing mix, so will have to share it out with care.

Dividing the budget

The marketing budget needs to be divided between the four areas of product, price, promotion and place. The product refers to the goods or services that are produced by the business. If the product is not good enough, no amount of promotion or pricing tactics will lead to its being successful so it is central to the mix. Price has to be set somewhere near the customer's perceived value for the product. A customer will have an idea of what a particular product should cost. While an airline ticket to New York could be acceptably priced at £300 it would be unlikely to get many takers at £3000. There will be a range of prices that the average consumer considers to be fair and reasonable for a product. The customer might be willing, in certain circumstances, to pay £600 or £700 for a seat on the plane, but is likely to be unwilling to pay more. Customers have an idea of '**value for money**' for a good or service. Promotion covers the various ways in which a business brings its product to the notice of the potential customer and tries to persuade them to buy it. This includes advertising, special offers, publicity stunts and other tactics. Place refers to where the product is sold, and how it gets there, so includes distribution.

Price

A key part of the mix is price. It is important to understand the basic relationship between price and demand. In general, the higher the price, the less a product will be demanded. Fewer people can afford it, and for many, it may fall outside their acceptable 'price range' or their idea of value for money. They may also switch to cheaper **substitutes**, if these are available. Lower prices, in general, encourage an increase in demand. Again, however, if a price drops too low, the customer might be suspicious of value. If a jeweller lowered the price of gold rings so that they were really cheap, customers would just assume that they were not gold!

> **Did you know...**
>
> There are also pricing 'tricks' such as psychological point pricing. This is where prices are deliberately set below certain 'trigger' prices such as £5 or £100. Prices seem a lot lower when they are £4.99 or £99.99 and promotions can claim the product is 'under a fiver' or 'less than a hundred pounds'.

Cost plus pricing

The most common form of pricing is probably cost plus pricing. This is where the business adds up the various costs of producing the good or service – raw materials components, power, labour, etc. and then adds on a percentage for profit (called a mark-up). Businesses will link mark-up to the price that they feel a consumer will be willing to pay for the product. If consumers see a product as having a high value (designer clothes, for example) then a big mark-up can be added to the actual costs of production. Most methods of pricing can be called competitive, as they involve pricing in such a way that a product sells at a similar price to those with which it is in competition.

Some customers will pay a high price for designer clothes

A price can be too low

Did you know...

Some pricing strategies are more promotional. A loss leader, for example, is where a product is priced so low that it does not even cover its costs. It is often a staple product (such as bread or milk) priced to attract customers into the shop so that they spend money on other products.

Summary

- The marketing mix is the mixture of factors needed in order to sell a product
- It has four parts: product, price, promotion and place
- The four parts are often referred to as 'the four Ps'
- Getting the right balance is more important than any one part
- The marketing mix will need to change over time, and as other factors change
- Price is a key part of the mix
- Price should be set to cover costs
- Customers have an idea of 'value for money; price must be set in this range

Marketing mix elements and price 71

Core knowledge

The business needs to keep an eye on all parts of the marketing mix, as the relative importance of the parts will change over time, particularly over the lifetime of a product. When a product is first launched, for example, it may be important to have a lot of promotion, to let customers know of its existence and where to buy it. Whatever is happening, some businesses will find it offers opportunities – even a hurricane makes work for roofers! As an example, let's look at three current trends that have been around for long enough to be regarded as established, and their possible effect on three businesses. Current trends include:

- a fall in the number of houses being built due to changes in the economy;
- trends towards more healthy eating and drinking habits;
- increased internet usage (and increased speeds through broadband).

Our three example businesses are a small building firm, a luxury restaurant and a local newspaper.

- The building firm needs to find new ways of finding work. Its excellent internet access, and the fact that planning applications are now published on the web, allows the owner to see when planning applications are approved. He can then promote his services to people who need them directly, using leaflets or even visiting.
- The restaurant could alter its product, by changing menus to healthier alternatives, organic produce and seasonal foods. It may also have to lower prices in order to attract different people.
- The local newspaper could change its product by carrying more advertising. It could also lower prices to advertisers. Increased advertising revenue could allow it to lower its cover price. Some newspapers are free, paid for by advertising.

And more

More important than allocating funds or efforts to each individual part of the mix is getting the balance right. The key to a successful business is not just a well-balanced marketing mix but one that is appropriate for the business and that responds appropriately to change. A small business could respond to a change in demand in a number of ways, depending on the change and on the type of business. If demand falls, a business may seek to revive sales by lowering price – knowing that lower prices should lead to an increase in demand. But there could be a catch. Some products are sold in very competitive markets, where it is easy for customers to switch from one seller to another. In these markets, the business is probably already charging the lowest price it can in order to compete. Lowering price could lead to lower profits, or even losses. It may therefore be better for the business to try to alter another part of the marketing mix. Perhaps new distribution channels could be opened, or changes made to the product. In other markets, the business may have a product that is so special and unique there is little competition, and there are no substitutes available. In this case, the business might be able to raise price and still not lose custom.

AQA BUSINESS FOR GCSE: SETTING UP A BUSINESS

Have a go

Group activity

Changes in a market bring some benefits and some drawbacks. Each person in your group should list three businesses which have gained from cheap air travel, and three that have lost. Decide which you think has lost the most. Decide on a pricing strategy to help them recover.

Discussion

The low cost, low price model used by Ryanair and easyJet has led to a lot more air travel taking place. Discuss whether or not increased air travel is a good thing or not, and why.

Web-based activity

List five current products that might go on your wish list for a birthday. Search the web to see how cheaply you could buy them. List the top and bottom prices for each product and note the difference. How much could you save by 'shopping around'? Explain why you think there is this difference in price.

Quickfire questions

1. What is meant by the 'Four Ps'?
2. What is the most important element of the marketing mix?
3. Why do small businesses have to be careful about marketing?
4. Why do different businesses have different marketing mixes?
5. What is meant by 'value for money'?
6. What is meant by a customer's 'price range'?
7. What happens to the marketing mix over time?
8. What usually happens to demand if price goes up?
9. What is cost plus pricing?
10. What is competitive pricing?

Hit the spot

▸ Define the marketing mix.
▸ Explain the link between 'price' and 'value for money'.
▸ Explain the relationship between price and demand. Under what circumstances might that relationship break down? Explain why you think so.

Cracking the code

Substitutes Products that can be bought instead of something, e.g. tinned fruit instead of fresh fruit.

Marketing mix The mixture or balance of the four key elements of marketing.

Value for money Nothing to do with the 'value' of the product, but linked to what the customer thinks it is worth; this may be different for different customers.

Chapter 13
Marketing mix elements and product

IN THE NEWS

The BBC iPlayer is a development of technology that the BBC was already running to allow people to listen to the radio over the internet. This takes up little bandwidth, and also allows users to listen to programmes that have already been broadcast, as well as listening to 'live' broadcasts. The iPlayer allows users with certain operating systems to download programmes, and watch them for up to 30 days. Other system users can watch TV programmes for up to seven days after broadcast, but not download them. Digital Rights Management (DRM) software is used to protect copyright and the commercial value of programmes so that they 'expire' after a set period of time and can no longer be played. Only users with a UK-based IP address can access the service, restricting it to Britain.

This version of the iPlayer was, when launched, only available to Windows XP users, leading to complaints that this was unfair to other users. A petition, sent to 10 Downing Street, demanded that the service be made available to people who did not use Windows. The petition reached over 16,000 signatures and brought a response from the BBC Trust (the governing body of the BBC) that: 'it noted the strong public demand for the service to be available on a variety of operating systems. The BBC Trust made it a condition of approval for the BBC's on-demand services that the iPlayer is available to

The BBC iPlayer

users of a range of operating systems, and has given a commitment that it will ensure that the BBC meets this demand as soon as possible.' By the Spring of 2008, the service was also available to Mac and Linux users and people using other browsers, such as Firefox and Safari.

The product has been a phenomenal success, and by 2008 was accounting for over 5 per cent of all internet traffic, and rising.

AQA BUSINESS FOR GCSE: SETTING UP A BUSINESS

> @ The BBC iPlayer can be found at www.bbc.co.uk/iplayer. Follow this link www.independent.co.uk/news/business/news/internet-groups-warn-bbc-over-iplayer-plans-461167.html and read the article published in *The Independent* newspaper. What changes do you think broadband providers are going to have to make to their product?
>
> Watch this 1958 Persil advertisement on YouTube at www.youtube.com/watch?v=L6880aSkS08. Has Persil made real or superficial changes?

> **Did you know...**
> Video streaming and internet rental has not succeeded in killing off the cinema. This is because the product they provide is different. Widescreen, surround sound and the 'experience' of cinema are not easily created in a home setting.

Responding to change

Businesses may fail or get into difficulty because they are unable to change their business model as circumstances change. It is important for businesses to be able to respond to change. They may be able to respond by changing any element of the marketing mix. Often it is most effective (and necessary) to change product. The BBC (and other broadcasters) had noted a significant change in demand so developed a new product in order to take advantage of this change.

Trends and markets

What they had seen happening in the market was a change in viewing habits, brought about by various advances in technology. The first change was the introduction of video recorders that could be programmed. These were used most often to 'time shift' programmes, so that people could watch them at times that were convenient to them. DVD recorders and 'Plus 1' channels, along with multiple repeats, also helped to drive this trend. At the same time, better and faster computer technology was allowing viewers to download films and video from the web. In 2006, Google launched a video service for people to buy video on demand, but it lasted less than a year, as the technology was not sufficiently developed. The BBC was the first to successfully develop a product that recognised viewers' changing habits and wants, and came out at the right time to make use of new technology.

Small businesses

Small businesses can learn many lessons from the BBC's success. They spent a long time getting the **product** right, and testing it in smaller markets, before going ahead with the national launch. The product itself has also had a knock-on effect on some small businesses, making the demand for video and DVD rentals fall.

Competition

Businesses need to be able to change in response to competition. If a competitor introduces a new

> **Did you know...**
> Businesses can make even better use of new technology through, for example, integrating different technologies. For example, you can programme your Sky+ box with a mobile phone if you've forgotten to do it at home.

Marketing mix elements and product

- The **product range** refers to the different product lines which a business sells. For example, the range in a bakers is likely to include bread, rolls, cakes, pastries and pies.

- The **product mix** refers to the variety of product types. A narrow mix means that the business is dependent on a particular market segment and so may be heavily affected by changes in that market. A baker who sells only bread products is not in as strong a position as one who also sells sandwiches, crisps and pies.

Technology

Businesses may also have to change a product due to changes in technology. When videotapes first became available, many specialist shops opened in order to provide rental services, which, as technology moved on, became DVD rental services. Now, some successful rental businesses have moved from physical premises to providing a postal service. The next stage is likely to be an internet only service, where films are streamed or downloaded. This will rely on appropriate technology being in place for consumers to download and pay for films and for producers to protect them from pirate copying.

New technology can change the market

product, or changes their product, then to stay successful the business will need to match this. Trends in markets will also mean that changes are necessary. Businesses can pick up current trends from press and media reports and, in their own industry, through specialist magazines (like *The Grocer*, *Farmers Weekly* and *Heating, Ventilating and Plumbing* magazine). Competing businesses that spot a trend or change first, and are flexible enough to be able to take advantage of it, tend to succeed. Businesses can change the product itself, the product range, or the product mix.

Changing the product is generally done by adding value – such as additional features or benefits. Sometimes these are real changes, sometimes only **cosmetic** (see 'And more' box).

> **Did you know...**
>
> Products are usually bought for a combination of core reasons and secondary reasons. The core reason for buying an item of clothing may be to stay warm. Colour and style give secondary benefits. A third layer of benefits comes from the promise of quality provided by the brand. This is known as the augmented product.

Summary

- Product is just one part of the marketing mix
- Businesses may respond to change by changing the product
- Some changes are caused by changes in technology
- Some changes are caused by competitors
- Businesses need to respond to changes by competitors
- Products can be changed by adding value
- Some changes are 'real' others may be cosmetic

Core knowledge

A product can be either a good or service. Goods are either for consumption or production. **Consumer goods** are either durable (lasting, like a car or freezer) or non-durable (quickly used up, like food, or toothpaste). Industrial or **producer goods** are those that are going to be used as part of the production process. These include tools, parts, factories and equipment. Services include services to individuals like haircutting, entertainment or car valeting and services that support business, like insurance, transport and banking.

Products go through a '**product life cycle**'. This describes the stages through which a product passes in a market. In the first stage, the product is researched and developed, before it is even brought to market. Many products do not survive this stage. Once the product is launched, it may need supporting with heavy promotion. If it is a good product, competitors will begin to bring out their own versions and the market can become crowded. At this point, changes can be made to the product to try to attract new markets, or to make it different to the competition. As long as further changes to the product can keep people buying it, this is worth doing, but with most products there comes a point when it is no longer worth the support, and it can then be allowed to die. In terms of time, product life cycles can be extremely short-lived – a matter of weeks – or carry on over a number of years.

And more

Customers buy products because of the benefits that they will get from them. These benefits are either real (or tangible) benefits or extra (or intangible) benefits. For example, buying (and wearing) an Adidas hat gives the real benefit of keeping your head warm. It also gives the extra benefit of you looking fashionable. Sometimes, the extra benefits are of more importance to a consumer than real benefits. A fashionable pair of shoes may not be as comfortable or as waterproof as unfashionable ones, but we may still prefer to wear them. The use of branding is a key way in which businesses try to make 'extra' benefits important. Where a business tries to make its product different to those of its competitors, this is called product differentiation. Big businesses can achieve this through the use of a brand.

Choosing style over comfort

Marketing mix elements and product

Changes to a product will also be of two types. There may be real changes, so that the product actually does perform better, or provide greater 'real' benefits. Increasing the power of a washing powder to clean or whiten would fall into this category. Other changes may be 'cosmetic'. Sometimes a product is repackaged or rebranded and not really changed at all. Calling something 'new' or 'improved' or saying it works 'better' is meaningless unless it is possible to compare performance. Putting it in a bag instead of a box, or a packet instead of a tin does not change the 'real' product and sometimes is an excuse to decrease value. A 'new, convenient size', for example, may disguise an increase in price.

Have a go

Group activity

Each person in your group should list three products that have been changed in order to increase demand. Look at all the products that you have listed between you and decide which change has been the most successful. Decide why you think this is the case.

Discussion

Look at the changes that have been made to Ariel over the years (see diagram). Which of these do you think are real changes and which cosmetic? Why do you think that soap powders, in particular, are always changing?

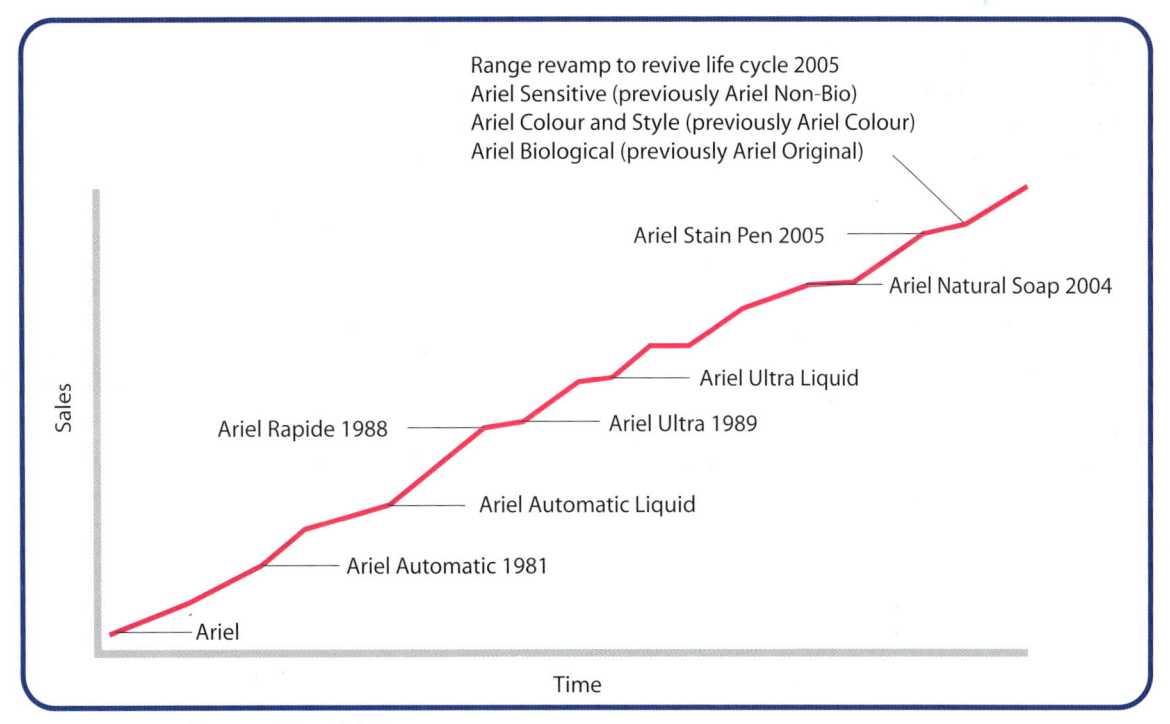

Graph showing sales over time with the following labelled points:
- Ariel
- Ariel Automatic 1981
- Ariel Automatic Liquid
- Ariel Rapide 1988
- Ariel Ultra 1989
- Ariel Ultra Liquid
- Ariel Natural Soap 2004
- Ariel Stain Pen 2005
- Range revamp to revive life cycle 2005
  - Ariel Sensitive (previously Ariel Non-Bio)
  - Ariel Colour and Style (previously Ariel Colour)
  - Ariel Biological (previously Ariel Original)

Revamping Ariel

AQA BUSINESS FOR GCSE: SETTING UP A BUSINESS

Web-based activity

List five current market changes that are affecting demand. Collect media cuttings or clips to illustrate your choice. Suggest which of these factors is having the biggest effect on demand, and for what. Suggest how this market could change its product (or another part of its marketing mix) to take advantage of the change.

Quickfire questions

1. Why is it important that a business can respond to change?
2. What is meant by a 'trend' in a market?
3. Name three current trends that could be important to a business.
4. What is the difference between a real change to a product and a cosmetic change?
5. What is meant by 'product range'?
6. What is meant by 'product mix'?
7. What is meant by 'adding value' to a product?
8. What is the difference between a good and a service?
9. What is meant by a 'consumer durable'?
10. What is a 'product life cycle'?

Hit the spot

> Define 'product' as part of the marketing mix.
> Explain why a wide product mix might be better than a narrow one.
> Which single part of new technology do you think has had the greatest effect on demand? Explain the reasons why you think this is the case.

Cracking the code

Consumer goods Those goods that are for consumption, i.e. to be used by customers.

Cosmetic Cosmetic changes are changes to the look or feel of a product that are basically surface changes, rather than a real change in the product.

Producer goods Those goods that will be used in production, like tools, machines, components.

Product The output of a business; what is produced for sale: this could be either a good or a service.

Product life cycle The stages a product passes through from research and launch to eventual withdrawal.

Product mix The variety of product lines offered by the business, therefore targeting several markets.

Product range The different product lines within a targeted market.

Chapter 14
Marketing mix elements and promotion

IN THE NEWS

Levi Roots ran a small business, on a limited budget, based on his grandmother's recipe and with production in his own kitchen. He operated as a sole trader, with limited capital, and limited opportunities for expansion. His opportunities to promote the product were – as with most small businesses – also fairly limited. His biggest sales were seasonal, made at the Notting Hill Carnival, which he had supplied with both music and Caribbean sauce for over 20 years. In fact, Levi's first career was as a musician, having played with some of the greats like Bob Marley, and being recognised at the MOBO awards. With the help of his seven children, Levi produced 65 bottles of the sauce a day in his kitchen. He packaged it himself and sold it at Brixton market, carrying it in a bag on his back. Demand from the Caribbean community became strong enough for Levi to set up a website to promote the sauce and take orders.

In 2006, Levi was spotted by a BBC researcher and invited to appear on *Dragons' Den*, the BBC programme where rich investors decide whether or not to support new ideas. Levi Roots sang his message to the entrepreneurs – the possible investors – and three pulled out straight away. Two – Peter Jones and Richard Fairleigh – could see the potential of the product and offered £25,000 each for a 20 per cent stake in the business.

Levi Roots and his Reggae Reggae Sauce

Within a few weeks of appearing on the programme, production had increased to 150,000 bottles a day and had to be moved to a factory. Peter Jones helped to secure a major order from supermarket Sainsbury's, and the sauce became its fastest selling brand, selling 40,000 to 50,000 bottles a week in over 600 stores.

What Levi Roots really needed was a promotional boost, to let the wider world know about his sauce. This came from the programme (which is watched by over 3 million people), so provided peak time advertising for a fraction of what it would cost on a commercial channel. His 'dragon' partners were also able to promote the sauce directly to big business, leading to its phenomenal success in a short space of time. Levi has also been able to use the success of the sauce, and his own talents for promotion, to promote his music career.

AQA BUSINESS FOR GCSE: SETTING UP A BUSINESS

> @ You can find Levi Roots' website at **www.reggae-reggae.co.uk/**. Look at this site and list the ways in which it covers all of the elements of the marketing mix.
>
> **http://video.google.com/videoplay?docid=-5382825371553385541&q**. This link takes you to a film of Levi talking and singing at an Enterprise event. What are the main points of his message to students?
>
> You will find seven promotion methods on this site: **www.canadaone.com/ezine/may99/promote.html**. Put them in order of which you think is most/least effective, and why.

Did you know...
The BBC does not carry any paid-for advertising. The BBC will often run promotional trailers for its own programmes, but will not accept advertising from commercial organisations. Instead the BBC is funded by government and the television licence fee.

Promoting a product

The product – Reggae Reggae Sauce – already existed, and was a good product. Levi Roots had already started to promote it, via his website. He also used the traditional promotional routes of the small business, such as recommendation and 'word-of-mouth' from satisfied customers. **Promotion** is just one part of the marketing mix, and it should be balanced against the other parts. It is no use having a huge budget for promotion and nothing left over for product development or distribution. The promotional methods chosen must be suitable for the business and the product that it is selling. Promotion is important but is also one area where the balance is sometimes wrong. A business can find that it has spent all of its money on promotion, but that there is no real effect on sales. Promotion can be expensive but, if it is not the right sort of promotion, can be ineffective. On the other hand, it is sometimes true that promotion that is free, or very cheap, can be just as effective as an expensive promotional campaign.

Above and below

Promotion consists of both 'above-the-line' and 'below-the-line' expenditure. **Advertising** is paid-for publicity for a product called 'above-the-line' expenditure. Other methods of promotion are called 'below-the-line' expenditure and include **public relations** and sponsorship. A suitable promotion method for a business will depend on the size of the business, the type and range of products that it is selling and on its market. A suitable budget for promotion should also be set, linked to:

- *Size*: A smaller business will obviously have less of a promotional budget than a larger one. This will limit it to certain media.

- *Products*: Some services can only be delivered personally. For example, you cannot sell a haircut to anyone other than the person in the chair! Industrial goods will be promoted through trained salespeople who can describe and demonstrate benefits at trade fairs and exhibitions or directly to the customer.

Did you know...
Some short-term prices are called 'promotional' prices, as they have been lowered temporarily. We recognise these through flashes saying 'sale' or 'reduced'.

Marketing mix elements and promotion

Small businesses

For a small business, the most suitable forms of promotion are likely to be:

- *Local newspapers*: these cover a precise geographical area so the business knows exactly who it is targeting. Using the government statistics site at **www.statistics.gov.uk** the business can carry out a postcode search and find out about the sort of customers that live in the area. Profiles will reveal house prices, average income, household size, patterns of expenditure and other information of use to a business. Just as important, perhaps, is the fact that such information is free.

- *Personal recommendation*: it is said that people tell ten others of every bad service experience they have, and just two of the good experiences. 'Word-of-mouth' is therefore very powerful and 'good reviews' are important.

- *Stationery and business cards*: these can carry product descriptions or be designed in such a way as to give a certain image to a business. Cards can also be placed in shop and newsagent windows and on notice boards.

- *Flyers, posters and leaflets*: online printing businesses have made these cheap to produce, but they still have to be designed and

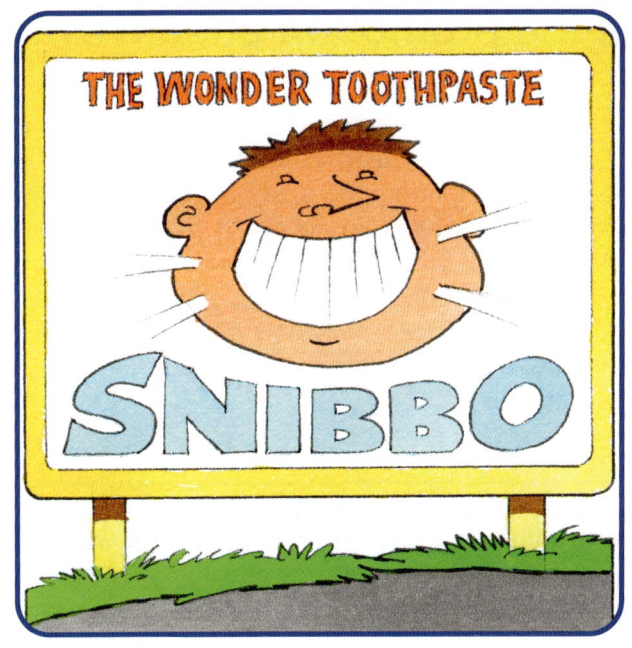

Advertising

- *Market*: Media are priced according to their 'reach', i.e. the number of potential customers reached. Many small businesses serve only a local market, so the use of TV, radio and national press advertising is not appropriate. The make up of the target market is also important. For example, if your product is aimed at teenagers, then promoting it to any other group is pointless.

Local sponsorship

distributed. Distribution can be targeted using postcodes.

- *Sponsorship*: this is available, but on a smaller scale. A business might, for example, sponsor the kit of a local or school football team, who then carry publicity on their kit.
- *Popular promotional techniques*: such as BOGOF (Buy One Get One Free) and other special offers can also be used by small businesses. They do, however, have to keep a very close eye on what these are costing them.

Is the promotion effective?

A business has to take all the costs and benefits of advertising into account when trying to see if a promotion has been effective. This is usually done by comparing the costs of the promotion with any increase in sales. It is not worth advertising if the benefits do not outweigh the costs. For example, if £1000 spent on promotion only resulted in £500 worth of increased sales revenue, then the promotion would be judged to be ineffective.

Did you know...

The main case in favour of advertising is that it informs – without it customers would not know what was on offer and would therefore not be able to make a choice. The case against advertising is that it is an unnecessary cost that is passed on to the consumer.

Summary

- Promotion is just one part of the marketing mix
- It consists of advertising and public relations
- AIDA (see Core) is the acronym used to remember what advertising should do
- Promotion is only effective if it is appropriate
- It needs to be appropriate to the size of the business, the type of product and the target market
- Small businesses can have effective advertising if they use the right media and hit the right target market

Core knowledge

Promotion covers all those methods that a business uses to communicate to consumers:

- that its product/s exist/s;
- that the product has features and benefits for the customer;
- that the customer should buy it.

The first aim is to make customers aware of a product. The second aim is to persuade consumers to buy it. The main ways in which businesses carry out these aims is through advertising and public relations.

Advertising is used to promote products through broadcast and print media of various types. **AIDA** is used as a way to remember the qualities that advertising should possess. It should attract

Sponsorship in action

Marketing mix elements and promotion

Attention; create Interest; develop Desire and lead to Action. Once advertising is successful in attracting attention, it can then create interest by telling customers about the benefits and features of a product. Businesses will try to convince the consumer that the product is something that they need, or will derive pleasure or use from. Once 'desire' has been created, the action of buying the product should follow.

Public relations is any way of generating publicity for a business. Methods include events, press conferences, sponsorship, endorsement and product placement. Sponsorship is used to link a product with a certain event, person or sport. A strawberry grower might wish to be associated with Wimbledon tennis for example. Endorsement is when someone well-known is persuaded to say or show that they think a particular product is worth having. Product placement involves giving products away to celebrities, or for use on films or television, in the hope that the product will be used on screen.

And more

Some new forms of advertising have emerged as new media has become more widely available. For example, a business may send advertisements directly to your mobile phone. A number of new ways of advertising also involve the internet. Internet sites carry banners for other sites that link to them directly by 'clicking through' and are rewarded every time a user is directed to the site. They may also carry other advertisements that load automatically before a page loads. These advertisements may be effective because they are bold and animated but may be ineffective if they cause irritation to the user.

Viral advertising relies on people to 'spread the word' to other people via the internet. This has now become a part of mainstream advertising campaigns. Businesses will set up fake websites or blogs that 'reveal' new products. The 'secret' word then spreads across the internet as people pass on the message. By the time the actual promotion is launched, there is already a huge level of interest. Viral advertising will reach yet another part of the market. For a small business, advertising on the internet is reasonably inexpensive. However, it may lead to problems of distribution. The internet is an international medium, so it should be made clear on the website of the business whether the business is willing to distribute its product outside the UK.

Have a go

Group activity

Each person in your group should list three advertisements that they have found persuasive, or amusing. For each one say what it was that was particularly good. Rank the advertisements in order and agree on which is the best, and why.

Discussion

Choose three recent advertisements that you think have been effective and, for each, say how well you think it fulfils 'AIDA'. Suggest ways in which each promotion could be improved.

Web-based activity

Find five major events or sports that are sponsored by businesses. Sporting examples could include cricket and football leagues, motor racing and golf. Events could include concerts and festivals. You could even find TV programmes and series that are sponsored. For each say why you think the sponsor backs the event and what benefits they will gain from it. Which do you think is the most effective, and why?

Quickfire questions

1. Describe 'above the line' promotion.
2. Describe 'below the line' promotion.
3. Name the two parts to promotion.
4. Name three sponsored events.
5. Name the three main factors that make for a suitable promotion.
6. What is meant by 'reach'?
7. Give one benefit of advertising in a local newspaper.
8. Why are postcodes important to small businesses?
9. How would a business judge if a promotion had been effective?
10. What does AIDA stand for?

Hit the spot

- Describe three suitable promotion methods for a small business.
- Explain the factors that are important in making a promotion suitable for a business.
- Using examples, explain why a particular business is sponsoring a particular event or sport. Judge whether or not the sponsorship is effective and say why you think so.

Cracking the code

Promotion That part of the marketing mix used to inform and persuade customers about products.

Advertising 'Above-the-line' promotion that is directly paid for.

Public relations (PR) 'Below-the-line' promotion – ways to attract attention and interest in a product that are not direct advertising.

AIDA The way to remember the qualities of effective promotion: it should attract Attention; create Interest; develop Desire and lead to Action.

Chapter 15
Marketing mix elements and place

IN THE NEWS

In April 2006 a music track by Gnarls Barkley made musical history by being the first to reach the Number One spot without selling any physical copies of the track. The track, called 'Crazy', was not released on tape or CD, single or album, but only as digital music, available via hugely successful music sites such as Apple's iTunes. It sold over 30,000 copies in a matter of hours, having already been made popular on Radio 1 as a jingle. It was bound to happen sooner or later as chart compilers and publishers decided that downloads had become so popular that they had to include them in the charts. They changed the rules so that this distribution channel was recognised as being as important as physical channels. After all, people were still buying the track, even if only digitally. Under the rule changes, as long as physical copies were going to go on sale up to a week later, downloads could count.

One month later Planet Funk used another 'new' distribution channel, made available by the growth of new technology, and released a track purely via mobile phone downloads. At the time, such downloads accounted for one in every 20 sales of tracks in the UK singles charts. '3', a mobile phone network, sold downloads at just 99p a track to both mobile phone and computer. 'I predict a riot' from the Kaiser Chiefs and 'Dare' from Gorillaz, each sold over 5000 copies once released via the mobile network.

Since then, many tracks have succeeded via downloads and it has become established as a new method of distribution. In other words, it is a new way to get the product to the consumer. The next step is to make even more use of the channel. Since downloads were made widely available, a number of illegal file-sharing or 'peer-to-peer' sites have appeared, where downloads of music are shared and therefore free. Producers do not want to lose the distribution channel, however, so are busy thinking up ways to make the product free, but also make money. In 2008, Universal, the world's largest recording company (home to the likes of Mariah Carey and U2) signed a deal to make millions of tracks available for free, on a site funded by advertising. The site (Qtrax) has also signed up the Beggars Group, the largest independent record producer in the UK (White Stripes, Radiohead, The Charlatans, Jarvis Cocker, Basement Jaxx) and industry giants Sony and EMI.

@

British group Coldplay hit the top of both the US and UK charts with a download-only single. Read about their success at: **www.mtv.co.uk/channel/mtvuk/news/23062008/426592/coldplay_top_both_charts**

Look at three websites, chosen at random. How do they fulfil the idea of 'place'? How will they distribute products to you?

> **Did you know...**
>
> Products can be pushed or pulled through the chain of distribution. A push strategy involves one part of the chain offering an incentive to the next part to take something from them. A pull strategy involves aiming incentives at the consumer who, by buying, pulls more products through the chain of distribution.

Finding the right place

The correct '**place**' (or mixture of places) and the ways to get a product to that place, will be linked to various factors. The most important of these are the product itself, the market at which it is targeted and the costs of **distribution**. In the case of a music track the product is easily transported but needs to be delivered quickly (and accurately), its target market is large, but easily accessed via technology, costs of distribution can be kept to a minimum. All businesses face the same decisions with their products.

Product

Products have different properties, all of which affect where they can be sold and how they are delivered. Look at the difference, for example, between coal and diamonds. Coal is heavy, bulky and dirty. Diamonds are small, valuable and clean. Neither has to be delivered with particular speed, but there are obviously security issues which make the transport of diamonds more expensive than coal. They will also be sold in very different places. Retail outlets range from the small, corner store or convenience outlet, up to huge hypermarkets and high street chains and department stores. Many still specialise in a particular product or line while others offer a more general range. Outlets need to consider which products will sell best, which offer the best profit margins and which products they actually have room to stock. Sales may need to be made in specialist surroundings, or with expert help, assistance or advice.

For neither of these products, however, is there a particular rush to reach a market. For something that is perishable, or new, this might be the prime concern. The first Beaujolais Nouveau of the season (a French red wine) is flown into the UK and sold at a high price; the first game birds shot at the start of the grouse season are delivered by helicopter to top London restaurants. Other foods may need to be processed or frozen. Transport may be arranged in such a way that the product arrives in a different condition, ready for sale. Bananas, for example, are packed into ships when still green, and ripen on the journey (they are too heavy and bulky to be flown).

Not the way to transport diamonds!

> **Did you know...**
>
> Distribution channels will be chosen by a business according to the most important factors affecting the product. Is it a good or a service? If it is a good, is it perishable, fragile, dangerous, large or valuable?

Marketing mix elements and place

new technology. They may also mistrust payment systems. On the other hand, making a product like a music track available via mobile phone and internet hits exactly the market at which it is aimed.

Costs

Distribution costs will depend on the size of the market and on factors linked to the product such as whether it needs to be delivered quickly, or securely, individually or in bulk amounts. Remember that 'place' is just one part of the marketing mix. If the distribution costs mean that price has to be increased, this may be enough to stop the product being viable.

E-commerce

Although businesses can create a website for what is essentially a very small outlay, they need to make sure that the site is properly built and maintained. There are costs involved in designing the site, hosting it, and maintaining it. The website may be the most 'public' part of the business, so it needs to be accurate and kept up-to-date. Internet sales are a growing market with many large grocery stores now offering an online service of ordering backed up by home delivery.

Bananas start their journey unripe

Market

The **target market** for the product may range from the very large – a mass market – to the very small – a niche market. Whatever the size of the market, the business has to consider how to reach it. It has to think about how the target market would access the product. For example, if the target market was older people, then making the product available via the internet would not be a good idea, as many older people do not use

Home delivery: orders are placed online

AQA BUSINESS FOR GCSE: SETTING UP A BUSINESS

Did you know...

Place is both distribution and the places where products are sold. It therefore includes outlets such as shops. There are also non-shop outlets such as direct sales, postal and internet sales and vending machines. Most industrial products, for instance, are sold by an agent, via direct sales. Other well-known products such as Tupperware are sold directly through party sales and Avon through door-to-door sales. Postal sales may be responses to mailshots or direct advertising or could be through mail order or catalogue sales.

Summary

- Place is just one part of the marketing mix
- The term 'place' refers to the place where a product is sold
- 'Place' also means the way that the product gets to that place: this is called distribution
- Distribution traditionally went through several phases – the long chain (see Core knowledge)
- Much shorter routes are now more popular
- The main factors that determine the right place and distribution are the product, its market and the costs of distribution
- E-commerce is a growing and important part of 'place'

Core knowledge

'Place' is one part of the marketing mix. It refers both to the premises or other outlets where a product may be sold and to distribution channels. These channels are the way that a product is delivered either to such outlets or directly to the final consumer. The traditional distribution strategy was via what was called 'long channel' distribution. This meant that the product followed a **chain of distribution** as follows:

producer → manufacturer → wholesaler → retailer → consumer

Each person in the chain tended to deal only with the person before or after them. Each also carried out a particular job. The wholesaler, for instance, bought large amounts, provided storage facilities and sold smaller amounts on to the retailer. The problem with such a long chain is that it is both costly and slow. Each person in the chain provides a service, and adds to the cost of the product as they take their fee. It can also take a product a long time to pass through all the stages. Shorter channels can be achieved by cutting out parts of this chain and the shortest channel is direct from producer to consumer. If this can also be achieved at little or no cost – as with digital downloads – this can make the product much cheaper than if it had to be transported to a shop from where the customer then bought it.

Marketing mix elements and place

And more

E-commerce refers to transactions that take place over the internet. To take place it needs a website – a place on the web where a potential customer can browse products and then buy remotely for delivery. It is a rapidly growing marketplace and as such yet another 'place' where products may be sold. There are two distinct and different routes into business on the internet. The first strategy is to set up as a pure 'dot com' business. This means that you only take orders via the web, and only distribute that way. One of the first companies to do this was Dell computers. This strategy gives access to a large market but removes the costs of shops, displays, sales staff and so on. The second strategy is to build on an existing successful business by adding an internet dimension. This is often referred to as 'bricks and clicks'. This is very much an area of growth and the majority of businesses now have a web presence. While the web may provide an inexpensive additional distribution channel, it should not be forgotten that most products still have to be delivered. The most successful web businesses are those that can sell the same product over and over again – commercial photo agencies, for example, or that provide a service that can be delivered via the web. These include advertising services, other services that can be carried out at a distance, such as share buying or tracing family histories and businesses that act as 'go-betweens', e.g. dating agencies, estate agencies and sites like Friends Reunited.

Have a go

Group activity

Each person in your group should choose three products at random. You could use catalogues or websites for this, or just rely on observation. Decide which product has the most costly distribution channel and list the reasons why.

Discussion

There is a huge market in illegal downloads – basically, people sharing music between each other, without paying for it. This is one of the reasons that downloads are now tending to be 'free'. Do you agree that this is the direction that music distribution should go in? Give reasons why you think so (or not).

Web-based activity

Find out all you can about Qtrax, such as who they have signed up and what tracks will be available. Explain how you think that their model of distribution will work.

AQA BUSINESS FOR GCSE: SETTING UP A BUSINESS

Quickfire questions

1. Describe the steps in traditional 'long chain' distribution.
2. Give an example of one retail outlet that is not a shop.
3. Name three properties that a product might have that would affect how it is transported.
4. Name three different types of retail outlet.
5. Name the three main factors that go to make up the correct 'place'.
6. What are the biggest and smallest markets called?
7. Give one advantage of using a website to sell products.
8. Give one disadvantage of using a website to sell products.
9. What does a wholesaler do?
10. What is meant by 'bricks and clicks'?

Hit the spot

> Describe how 'place' is an important part of the marketing mix.

>> Explain how and why distribution for a mass market will need to differ from that for a niche market.

>>> Choose three products. For each product suggest one appropriate and one inappropriate 'place' to sell it. Justify your suggestions by referring to the product, its market and the costs of distribution.

Cracking the code

Chain of distribution The stages that a product passes through from producer to consumer.

Distribution The part of place that deals with making the product available to the consumer.

Place The part of the marketing mix that refers to where a product is sold and how it gets to that place.

Target market That part of a market at which the product is aimed.

FINANCE

SECTION 4

Chapter 16
Sources of finance

IN THE NEWS

The National House Building Council reported in Spring 2008 that housing starts were well down on the previous year. Over 20,000 houses were started in May 2007, with around three-quarters of these in the private sector. By May 2008 this had fallen to 9600, a fall of around 60 per cent. The fall has affected big and small businesses alike.

Taylor Wimpey is one of Britain's biggest building firms. It was formed in 2007 through the merger of Taylor Woodrow and Wimpey. Despite its size, it has still been hard hit by the 'double whammy' of increased credit costs and a declining housing market. It is in an industry where borrowing and debt is important. Houses and flats have to be built before they can be sold, so payments for land, labour, materials and services have to be made before any revenue can be collected from house sales. On small building sites, where only a few houses are being built, costs are often not recouped until the last house is sold. On bigger sites, there may be a 'rolling programme' of sales, with 'Phase 1' sales being used to finance 'Phase 2', and so on. Those building commercial properties like offices and shops are no better off – they still have to find businesses to rent the space. Taylor Wimpey has had to take action to bring its costs down and has cut 600 jobs while closing 13 of its regional offices. It has also stopped expanding, put some developments on 'hold' and put off starting new ones. The company has almost £2 billion of debt, held against its assets (what it owns). The trick is to keep lenders confident so that the debt can be managed.

Craig and Sean Deering both followed their father into the building trade. They are builders on a much smaller scale than Taylor Wimpey but face the same sort of problems. Deering Brothers Builders has debt held on credit cards and through trade accounts with their local building supply agency. They also have a business bank loan with monthly repayments that have to be met. To stay in work, as the housing market contracted, they have used some of their own savings to continue projects. They have also been forced to dramatically reduce the price of the houses they are building. As Sean says, 'We have a lot of debt, but hope that we can keep on top of it until the market picks up.'

@ Visit the Bank of England's site at **www.bankofengland.co.uk** to find out the latest figures for interest rates and for inflation. Work out what effect these will have on the housing market. Why is this important?
Visit estate agents' websites in your area. What can you tell about the housing market from these sites?
Look at **www.angelsden.com**. Would this be a suitable place for a business to look for finance? Can you say why you think so?

Sources of finance

> **Did you know...**
>
> Companies often promise to carry debt only up to a certain percentage of the value of their assets. For example, on assets of £100,000, they might promise to hold just £5,000 (5 per cent) of debt. The problem comes when the value of the asset – for builders this is often land – is written down. If, in our example, the value drops to £90,000, the percentage is now above 5 per cent, so the business has broken its promise.

How much? Where from?

Probably the most frequently asked question for the small business start-up is 'Where do I get the money from?' The answer to the question generally comes in two halves. Firstly, before deciding on possible sources for the finance, how much do I need? Only then can the entrepreneur begin to look for suitable sources. The 'how much?' needs to cover fixed costs, variable costs and any possible **contingencies** (things that might happen in the future). Details of these are covered in Chapter 19. Small businesses will not have shareholders and, while they may have the option to become a private limited company, raising money via a stock exchange issue is not a route that is open to them.

Small businesses

For many small businesses the major form of finance will be the **owner's own funds**. These will come from personal savings and income. The owner may also raise money from friends and family, without the need for any formal agreement or payment of interest. It is up to them if they want to risk their money! These funds may also include the profits of the business. Profits that are kept for this purpose are called '**retained profits**'.

In addition, businesses will have to borrow money. This may be short term, to cover immediate payments, medium term, or long term to cover expensive items that are going to take a long time to pay for.

Short-term loans

Short-term loans are usually measured in terms of weeks or months, or even just days. While these are obviously short term, anything up to a maximum of three years is also considered to be short term. Sources for such loans are banks, or through various forms of credit. The main short-term borrowing from banks is through overdrafts or loans.

- An **overdraft** is when the bank allows a business to take more out of a current account than it has in it. It is a flexible way to borrow as the business can borrow as much or as little as it needs up to the overdraft limit. The business only pays interest on the amount of money actually borrowed at any time.

- A loan is a fixed amount borrowed over a set period. The business would borrow the whole amount it needed, and then pay this, and the interest, in set instalments. It is not as flexible as an overdraft but can be better for a business wanting to keep control of its budget as the business knows exactly how much it needs to pay and when.

> **Did you know...**
>
> Credit may be formal or informal. With formal credit agreements, there is a written contract. Informal agreements are very common in small business communities. Goods may be taken 'on trust' and it is the reputation of the business that is the guarantee that repayment will be made.

Medium-term loans

Medium-term finance is defined as loans taken out over a period of between three and ten years. Medium-term loans are likely to be used to buy fixed assets such as machines and vehicles. The bank will often have a call on the particular asset as security for the loan. This means that if the business fails, or cannot pay for the loan, the bank can take the asset and sell it.

A delivery vehicle is an asset

Long-term loans

Long-term finance is reckoned to be loans from ten years upwards. These are usually taken out from banks that specialise in commercial loans. The alternative is to go to a bank or building society and take out a mortgage on factories, land or property. A **mortgage** is a long-term loan with property or land as **security**.

Venture capital

Businesses may also be able to take out loans from private investors. Successful entrepreneurs may wish to back a particular business venture if they think that it will be a success. They may also want to take part in running the business. This source is known as 'venture capital' and the individuals who provide it are often known as business 'angels'.

Finance may also be raised through government grants or related schemes. These are covered in the next chapter.

Did you know...

Debt is not a problem for most businesses as long as it can be managed. Actually borrowing money, or using credit, is a necessary step for the majority of businesses. Problems only arise if payments are not made, or the business cannot afford the interest. It is vital for a business to manage its debt properly.

Sources of finance

Summary

- The main source of finance for a small business is the owner's own funds
- Issuing shares is not an option for the small business
- Most businesses need to borrow funds, or use credit
- Borrowing will be for the short, medium or long term
- Overdrafts provide flexible short-term borrowing
- Medium-term borrowing is usually secured against an asset
- Long-term borrowing is often in the form of a mortgage
- Trade credit is a common way for businesses to borrow
- All borrowing comes with a cost attached
- Borrowing is necessary for most businesses, what is important is that the debt is properly managed

Core knowledge

Small businesses have to use whatever sources they can for finance. While these businesses can apply for overdrafts or loans, small businesses and new businesses often have great difficulty in raising the money that they need. This is because the future for many businesses is uncertain. They can have a good idea, or what they think is a good product, and still not be a success. Banks and building societies know the failure rate of small businesses and may therefore be very careful about the loans that they make to them – or put strong conditions on them. Sometimes the conditions – such as high interest rates, or wanting security on the assets of a business – are enough to put the business off. Many entrepreneurs setting up a new business find that the most reliable source of finance is their own savings. They may also borrow from friends and family who are willing to take the risk. Banks and other lending institutions will want much more solid guarantees as they have the interests of their own depositors and shareholders to take into account. Entrepreneurs may also raise money on those assets that they already own. A householder can remortgage a house, for instance, in pursuit of a business dream.

Re-mortgaging the house can fund a business start-up

Businesses can find it easier to raise money if they have a clear business plan, good market research and a really good idea of the amount of risk involved. Of course, if they are successful, there will be high levels of reward – but what happens if the business is not a success?

AQA BUSINESS FOR GCSE: SETTING UP A BUSINESS

> **And more**
>
> One way for a business to raise finance is through various forms of credit. Credit is, essentially, borrowing something and paying for it later. It is a form of loan, but one that will have different conditions and costs to a bank loan. Credit may come through the trade, through using credit cards or through buying machinery, vehicles, tools or other capital equipment on **hire purchase**.
>
> Trade credit is common in a number of industries. Small building firms, like the Deerings, will have agreements with building trade suppliers so that they can collect material, timber, sand, cement and so on as and when they need it, settling up at the end of the month or another pre-agreed period, Such credit is often free – it helps the suppliers to keep sales up and helps the buyers to budget. In other businesses, for example retail, stock may be bought on credit. This is because the trader hopes to have sold the stock before it must be paid for. In some cases stock is bought on a 'sale-or-return' basis. If the business can't sell it, it is sent back and does not have to be paid for. Small or new businesses may also use credit cards to finance their purchase of stock. If very carefully managed, this can provide an interest free way of borrowing money. To be interest free, the business would have to pay off all of what is owed by the monthly due date. While this can provide up to 56 days of free credit, the penalties for failing to pay it off are extremely high, with interest rates way above those of a bank loan.

Have a go

Group activity

The BBC TV programme *Dragons' Den* is all about venture capital. Watch an episode (you may have to find one on the web) so that you can see the process. Your group will then act as the 'dragons' for another group, who will pitch an idea to you. Then reverse the roles of the groups.

Discussion

Why do small businesses often have trouble raising the finance they need? Decide on a number of key steps that a business should take in order to make the raising of finance an easier process.

Web-based activity

Find out all you can about business angels and venture capital. (You could start at www.angelsden.com). If you were a small business, how would you go about raising venture capital?

Sources of finance

Quickfire questions

1. Define 'owner's funds'.
2. What is meant by 'retained profit'?
3. Give three personal sources of finance for a small business entrepreneur.
4. Give one example of short-term borrowing.
5. Give one example of medium-term borrowing.
6. Give one example of long-term borrowing.
7. Define what is meant by 'security' in financial terms and give an example.
8. What is a mortgage?
9. Why do people make venture capital available?
10. What is meant by trade credit?

Hit the spot

> Outline the costs that a business will have to take into account before looking for funds.

> Explain the difference between an overdraft and a loan. Give examples of when each would be appropriate.

> What could be the role of venture capital in small business finance? Would it be a good idea for a small business to seek venture capital? Give reasons for your answer.

Cracking the code

Contingencies Events that might cause costs in the future. A single one is a contingency.

Owner's own funds The owner's personal money.

Retained profits Profit kept from previous trading by a business.

Overdraft Permission to take more from a current account than is deposited.

Mortgage A long-term loan with property or land as security.

Security An asset that can be sold to repay a loan.

Hire purchase Buying something on instalments over a period of time.

Chapter 17
Business support

IN THE NEWS

The Prince's Trust is one of a number of bodies that helps young people, including helping them into business. It concentrates on those who have had a rough deal – perhaps with disabilities, or failing at school, or from difficult family backgrounds. Much of its success is due to the support that it receives from the business communities where it operates. The Trust provides grants, advice and support to 18 to 30 year olds who need it. Its annual Celebrate Success Awards showcase success around the country.

- In Yorkshire, Oliver Griffiths, 24, unemployed, housebound and in a wheelchair, approached The Prince's Trust to set up a business helping young people into sport. A grant enabled him to attend coaching courses and then run courses for both able bodied and disabled youngsters. He also provides sports coaching for young people, both with and without disabilities.
- In London, Cat Byshiem, 29, was helped to set up Catherine Byshiem Jewellery Design. Originally from Norway, she designs jewellery based on Norwegian culture, patterns and stories. Her work has become well known enough for her to form part of a jewellery trade visit to New York. She received not just money from the Trust, however, but perhaps more importantly, support from two business mentors – successful business people who volunteer their services to help and advise young entrepreneurs.
- In the Midlands, Nyree Clark studied animal care at college but could not see how to turn this into a business until advised by the Trust. Again, it was not just money that was offered by the Trust, but sound business advice that led to her setting up Clark's Pet Couriers, offering a range of pet-related services. She now works with a number of local vets and has a small fleet of specialist vehicles for transporting pets.
- In the West Country, Claire Foster, 27, from Taunton, looked for a way of finding success on the back of the increase in demand for healthy food and drink. She saw that the market for smoothies was expanding, so set up a mobile juice bar called Superjuice. Set up with a grant from the Prince's Trust in 2005, it has expanded to include a hot range of healthy soups, porridge and even hot juices.
- In Norwich, Chinelo Brown was helped to set up a hair and beauty salon specialising in Afro-Caribbean styles. Starting with Chinelo's Hair Salon in 2006, it has already expanded into a high street beauty salon offering a range of services to men and women.

Business support

@ **www.businesslink.gov.uk** links to all parts of the UK governments business support network.
Follow the link to 'events' and see if you can find an event in your area that you could visit.
Listen to Claire Foster, owner of Superjuice, talking to *Dragons' Den* star Deborah Meaden on this link:
video.google.com/videoplay?docid=-8187285306371784895&hl=en. What do you think of Deborah's ideas? What would you suggest yourself?
Visit **startups.co.uk** and click through 'entrepreneurs' to 'young entrepreneurs'. Choose which of the examples you think is the most enterprising, and say why.

Did you know...
Informal support – that of friends and family, and of people you know with experience in business – can be just as useful as the formal support offered by organisations. For example, local knowledge of marketing opportunities may come from a friend or relative, rather than any official resource.

Organised support

Support organisations, like the Prince's Trust, can help businesses in all stages of their development. The Prince's Trust (Prince's Youth Business Trust (PYBT), to give it its full name) provides grants and other assistance to young people under the age of 30 wanting to set up in business. It can help in market research, to find markets, and to develop products and services. Some bodies offer financial support. Others, just as importantly, offer advice and experience. Each successful business listed above was helped by an experienced business **mentor**. These are people with business knowledge who volunteer their time in order to support young people setting up new businesses. Many commercial organisations offer free advice and support as it is in their interest to have businesses run efficiently. High street banks, for example, will advise businesses on handling finance, and Citizens Advice Bureaux advise about business and employment regulations. The two main areas of business support are in finance and advice.

Advice and assistance

The government has a number of schemes in place which are designed to help small businesses. The Business Start Up Scheme, for example, is partnered with the Prince's Trust and is focused on deprived areas. It is aimed at helping the long-term unemployed find work through starting their own business. A visit to the business link site (**www.businesslink.gov.uk**) will show you that there are nearly two and a half thousand grants and support schemes available, as well as a wide range of training courses for both businesses and their staff. These include local, regional and national schemes as well as grants and support from outside bodies such as the European Union. Other bodies may encourage businesses of a particular type or group – such as The Arts Council for arts based businesses. Certain parts of government will also help with specific problems. HM Revenue and Customs will advise on taxation and customs rules, UK Trade and Investment will advise on overseas markets, the UK Intellectual Property Office (UKIPO) will advise on designs, trademarks, **patents** and **copyright**.

Did you know...
The government provides a series of guides to funding, finance and support. These can be accessed through the **businesslink.gov.uk portal**. They are free to download.

An experienced business person can be a helpful mentor

Funding

The government helps by encouraging banks and other financial institutions to lend money to businesses. The Small Firms Loan Guarantee scheme helps those businesses that have a good business idea, but do not have the assets to offer a bank as security. In this case, the government will guarantee up to 75 per cent of the loan, should the business fail.

In March 2008, as part of the Budget Report, a new Enterprise Strategy was launched. It is designed to help both new and existing businesses get the funding they need. It also helps businesses to understand and cope with business rules and regulation. The Strategy's central vision is to make the UK the most enterprising economy in the world and the best place to start and grow a business. It has five key aims:

- To create a culture of enterprise – where everyone who can be an entrepreneur is inspired to take up the challenge. There should be no barriers of age, gender, race or social background.

- To promote enterprise as a life-long journey, from primary school, through secondary school and into higher education.

- To provide access to funds so that entrepreneurs and small business owners can access the finance they need.

- To reduce and simplify the laws that govern businesses, to make this area easier to cope with.

- To help people to innovate, i.e. to develop new ideas and products.

Anyone who has an idea for a new or improved product, process or market can become an entrepreneur

Did you know...

If you are researching and developing a new product, your business may be allowed to set off some of the costs against tax. The government wants to encourage innovation, so provides **tax relief** in this area.

Business support

Summary

- There are many ways in which small and new businesses can gain support
- The majority of support is free
- Support may come in the form of advice or finance
- Advice is available formally and informally, locally, regionally and nationally
- The government has set up a network of websites and publications to provide advice
- Support may be available to help a business find finance through loans
- Financial support may also be available through grants
- Government is 100 per cent committed to enterprise, and therefore to supporting business

Core knowledge

Often the first place for a new business to visit will be the Local Authority where it is based. This will have a business support unit that can help it directly, or can put the business in touch with local Chambers of Commerce, Business Link or the Learning and Skills Council (LSC).

Chambers of Commerce are local organisations, made up of local businesses of all sizes and types. They link together to make a national network that will help and support business. British Chambers of Commerce (BCC), the national group, represents businesses that employ over 5 million people. Support is provided either from the national body, or at a local level. For example, to help new businesses BCC has developed a business start-up pack (**www.thebusiness-startup.co.uk**). Your local Chamber of Commerce can be found and accessed through **www.britishchambers.org.uk**. Chambers of Trade are similar locally based organisations.

Business Link is the government website that has been set up to help new business. Its sections include advice on starting up, finance and grants, employment, health and safety and taxation as well as advice on marketing, using e-commerce tools and expanding the business once it is established.

The LSC (Learning and Skills Council) can help the entrepreneur by providing the appropriate training – either to the owner or to employees. This includes access to an Adult Learning Grant. This is especially important for people who want to learn about new technology and how it can help their business to succeed.

> ### And more
>
> While businesses may have to borrow money or use their own funds, finance may also be raised through government grant or related schemes. The Grants and Support Directory (on **www.businesslink.gov.uk**) can be searched for grants specific to your area (such as rural businesses, or women into business) and to particular problems or issues – such as marketing, product development or expansion.
>
> A grant is, in effect, a gift of money to a business. there is no interest, and the money does not have to be repaid. There are, however, fairly strict rules governing whether a grant may be available or not, and the application process may be complicated. It is also likely that certain conditions will have to be met (a minimum number of employees, for instance, or the grant may only be available to certain types of business). There is also likely to be competition for the grants available. Many grants involve '**matched funding**' where the grant is made only up to the amount of funding that the business is able to raise and risk itself. Grants may be made by national or local government and in such cases are often linked to particular areas where the government feels that help is needed. This may include areas of high unemployment (perhaps because a major local employer has failed) or government designated Enterprise Areas. There are 2000 Enterprise Areas in the UK situated in the most deprived areas of the country.

Have a go

Group activity

Go to the government's business link site (**www.businesslink.gov.uk**) and choose one of the support schemes available. Write a paragraph to explain the scheme. Make a leaflet to tell a local business about the various schemes by putting your paragraphs together. You should make it as attractive as possible, but also make sure that the advice is clear and accurate.

Discussion

Why do you think that the government is promoting a 'culture of enterprise'? What benefits will it bring to the economy? Are there any drawbacks?

Web-based activity

Visit the website of the UK Intellectual Property Office (UKIPO) at **www.ipaware.net/members/ UKIPO.htm** and describe the process you would have to go through to register a new design or idea. How do you think that this helps new businesses?

Business support

Quickfire questions

1. What is meant by a grant?
2. What is the PYBT?
3. Give three sources of free advice for a business.
4. What is meant by 'tax relief'?
5. Describe the Business Start Up Scheme.
6. What is UKIPO and what does it do?
7. What is a Chamber of Commerce?
8. What is the LSC? What does it do?
9. What is a patent? How does it help a business?
10. What is meant by 'matched funding'?

Hit the spot

- Describe the work of the Prince's Trust.
- Explain how the Small Firms Loan Guarantee scheme works.
- Support for new businesses can come in the form of funds – money – or advice from experienced business people. Which of these do you think is most important? Give reasons for your answer.

Cracking the code

Copyright Protection of the written word from being copied.

Matched funding When the business is expected to put in the same amount as a grant – so that for every £1 of grant, the business matches this funding. In this way, the business is half funded by grant and half by the business.

Mentor Person with business knowledge who helps to guide businesses.

Patent Protection from copying for an original design.

Tax relief When the government decides not to take tax on certain earnings.

Chapter 18
Keeping accounts

IN THE NEWS

Business Active is a colour print magazine aimed at students, like you, studying business, finance or economics. For the magazine to be in profit means that it would have to take enough in revenue to cover all of its costs. This sounds easy, but, for Business Active, there were many costs to take into account and only limited sources of revenue. For a publication, there are generally two possible revenue streams. These are the cover price of the magazine or newspaper, and advertising revenue. For many publications the most important of these is advertising revenue, and a large proportion of a publication will be taken up by advertisers. With some publications, there is so much advertising that the publication can be free and is given away. Many local newspapers follow this model. With Business Active being aimed at an educational market of 14–16 year olds, however, its owners did not feel that advertising was appropriate. This left them with just the one revenue stream and the problem of finding the right price to attract buyers.

Costs, however, were another matter. Some costs are linked to the production of the magazine, others to promoting it or distributing it. The magazine has to be written, designed and typeset, and photographs taken and inserted. This means payments to writers, designers, photographers and administrative staff. It has to be printed, meaning payments to printers, and it has to be distributed, meaning payments to a firm of packagers and finishers, and postal charges. But even before all of this, there are other costs, some of which may never be recovered. These include initial advertising, a mailshot (written, designed, printed and posted) to all 5600 secondary schools in the country. This is expensive, but no sales have yet been made, so this involved borrowing the money and therefore incurring another cost – interest.

Whether or not the magazine reaches its sales target makes little difference to those from whom office space is rented, or who provide telephone or other communications services. They will have to be paid however many copies are sold.

Without proper accounts it is impossible to see whether the magazine is in profit or not or where improvements can be made to try to make it more successful, or more profitable. Clear and accurate accounts are an essential part of running even the smallest business.

Keeping accounts

@ Visit your local estate agent's website and see how much it would cost to rent or buy a small office. What other costs do you think a business would face once they had chosen a property?
Choose a small business type that you might like to open. (Perhaps a hairdressers, or nail bar, perhaps a small builder or retail business, perhaps a computer-based business.) List everything that you will have to buy to set up. Search the web for suppliers and see what the total costs of your set-up will be.
Look at **www.hsbc.co.uk/1/2/business/finance-borrowing/business-loan** or a similar site and work out how much your loan will cost you. Remember, interest payments are a cost!

Did you know...
It is almost possible, with new technology, to be completely mobile. You could operate an internet service from a laptop. In this case your 'land' is anywhere that you set the laptop down to use it. Of course, this may make the 'land' element free or very low cost.

Business accounts

Many businesses struggle to survive because they do not keep a proper account of how much is being spent and how much received. This sounds like such a simple thing that it is difficult to see how a business could overlook it. However, particularly with a small or new business, there may be many, many other jobs which are, or seem to be at the time, more important than recording income and expenditure. It is vital, however, that a business keeps track of what is going out, as well as what is coming in!

Revenue

A business would not be in business unless it was taking money. The cash that it takes is called sales **revenue**. It is measured as the price of a product multiplied by the number of sales. A common mistake is to confuse revenue with **profit**. Revenue just measures the money coming in from sales, and takes no account of cost. Imagine buying a magazine for £2.50 and then selling it to a friend for £2. You have a revenue of £2, but have actually lost 50p on the deal. Revenue is the income a business receives for the sale of its goods or services. There could,

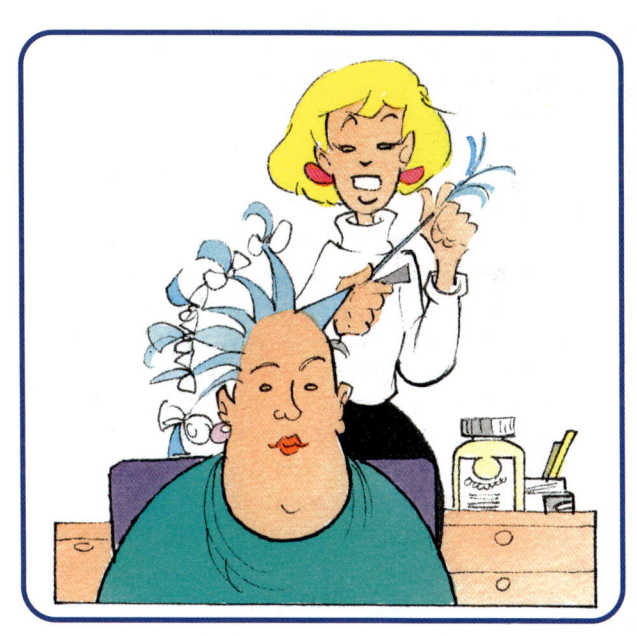

A small business owner must keep track of income and expenditure

Did you know...
One of the areas that makes keeping accounts difficult is that values do not stay constant. A machine or vehicle is worth more when it is first bought than six months or a year later. This fall in value is known as 'depreciation'. Eventually, what was once a brand new shiny asset will be worth nothing!

The assets of a business will include vehicles, stock, buildings, machinery, etc.

therefore, be several streams of revenue for a business from the different products and services that it offers. A magazine, for example, will have revenue from its sales of copies and its sales of advertising space.

Resources

Whatever the type of business, it will require certain resources in order to operate. These are referred to as 'factors of production'. Every business needs

- *Land* – meaning somewhere from where to operate the business; this may be a space to put a factory, store goods or park vehicles. Equally, for a small business, it could refer to the back bedroom being used as office space. You may think that somewhere like a mobile hairdressers doesn't need land, but you would be wrong. Whatever the business, it needs a 'home base', and even a mobile business has to have a fixed point to which mail is sent.
- *Labour* – someone to actually do the work. In the smallest businesses the labour is provided by the owner himself or herself. Whatever this person does, is counted as labour. So this includes planning and thinking along with anything physical. Obviously, in larger businesses, there will also be people employed. Also included in 'labour' can be the original ideas, innovation and hard work that goes into 'enterprise'.
- *Capital* – this is not money (although often wrongly referred to as money) but the **assets** of the business – machinery, vehicles, buildings, raw materials, tools. Even brands and things like reputation can have a figure put on them.

Wages, power and telecoms bills are running costs

Costs

All of these inputs cost money and so have to be accounted for. A typical business has rent or mortgage payments on premises, business rates and **costs** for power and communications. It has wages to pay (even in one-person businesses, where the owner needs to include his or her own 'wage' in the accounts). It has to pay for materials and other costs of producing its product. Some of these costs only need to be paid once, others keep having to be paid.

- **Start-up costs** are also called sunk costs. These are costs that have to be met before the business can start to produce its good or service. They include buying machinery, furniture, vehicles and office and other equipment. They might also include market research costs and initial marketing.
- **Running costs** are those costs that have to be paid to keep the business operational. Examples include raw materials, wages, power and telecoms bills. Some start-up costs become running costs, e.g. if the business buys a machine on credit, the initial deposit is a start-up cost, the continuing payments are running costs. Running costs have to be paid, or the business cannot function. Once the business is covering its running costs, any additional revenue can go towards offsetting the start-up costs.

Did you know...

Another way to divide costs is into 'fixed' and 'variable' costs. Fixed costs have to be paid whether or not the business is producing anything. Examples include rent and the fixed part of power bills. Variable costs are directly linked to production, such as the amount of paper or ink used to produce a magazine.

Summary

- Keeping accurate accounts is vital to the efficient running of a business
- All businesses receive revenue from sales
- Revenue is not profit
- All businesses have certain costs
- Businesses have to pay for their inputs: these are land, labour and capital
- Some costs are paid at start-up, before the business can operate
- Some costs are ongoing, and are called running costs

Core knowledge

You can practise the skills of accounting by drawing up a simple budget for yourself. This is a good way to plan spending and make sure that you can afford what you want. Like a business, you will have certain sources of income. You are probably not selling a good or service, so this is income, rather than sales revenue. (The minute you do sell something for money, it becomes sales revenue, and you are operating a business, even if it is only making cakes and selling them at the school fair.) Like a business, you could have different sources of income – perhaps some of it is earned: pocket money for doing jobs around the house, a paper round, a part-time job. Some of it will be gifts rather than earned (and may be irregular) such as birthday money or money for passing examinations. You will also have expenditure, again in various different ways. Some of your spending may be regular (like the rent or fixed power charges that a business has to pay). Some may be extraordinary 'one off' spending – buying an expensive present for a special birthday or occasion, for instance. Other spending may be regular – payments into a savings account, magazine or club subscriptions, bus or train fares or other travel costs. Some may go up or down unexpectedly. For instance, a problem or crisis (or even a new relationship) may cause you to use your mobile phone much more than usual. You can see from this that your own income and expenditure is complex, so it is no wonder that a business may find it even more so.

And more

In business, there are two different kinds of account, and therefore two different kinds of accountant. The difference is between those accountants who work with the figures produced now and in the past, and those who have the job of predicting and forecasting what might happen in the future. The first group are called financial accountants. These are in charge of accurately recording the costs and revenues of a business. They prepare the figures, balances and accounts to help the business to operate efficiently. In a small business set-up, such as a sole trader or partnership, these accounts could be quite simple. They are important for two sets of people – the tax authorities and the owners themselves. The tax authorities need to know how much income is earned so that they can charge income tax on individuals and corporation tax on profits. The owner needs to know so that they have a clear picture of what is happening in the business, and know if they need to cut costs or boost revenue.

Once a business becomes a limited company, there is a legal requirement to publish certain figures. These include balance sheets, showing a snapshot of what a business owns and owes at any one time, a profit and loss account, and, in public limited companies, a statement to show the flows of cash in and out of the company. These are all figures that relate to the past performance of the business.

The second group are called management accountants. These use internal business figures for forward planning. (See page 120.)

Have a go!

Group activity

Each of you should draw up a set of three 'rules' for a small business in terms of how and when to keep accounts. Put all the rules together and agree on the most important 'top five'. You could then draw up a leaflet or poster to illustrate these.

Discussion

Why do you think so many businesses – particularly small businesses - find it hard to keep accurate and up-to-date accounts? List the reasons and possible solutions. Suggest good practice that would help a business person.

Keeping accounts

Web-based activity

Use a spreadsheet to draw up a simple budget for yourself for the next six months. Use a search engine to find an online guide to your programme and make it interactive, so that you can change income and expenditure and see what happens.

Quickfire questions

1. Describe what is meant by 'revenue'.
2. Describe what is meant by 'profit'.
3. Name a business. Give three possible costs for this business.
4. Give one possible source of revenue for this business.
5. Define what is meant by 'land' as a factor of production.
6. Define what is meant by 'labour' as a factor of production.
7. Define what is meant by 'capital' as a factor of production.
8. What is an asset?
9. What is the difference between start-up and running costs?
10. Name the two different kinds of accountant.

Hit the spot

- Explain the difference between revenue and profit.
- Which is the most important factor out of land, labour, capital and enterprise? Give reasons for your choice.
- Explain the difference between start-up costs and running costs. Which is most important to a business? Give reasons for your choice.

Cracking the code

Asset What the business owns, such as stock or equipment or vehicles.

Costs A precise business term, referring to the amount that has to be paid for a good or service that a business needs. Costs are then further subdivided.

Profit The difference between cost and revenue, when revenue is greater than cost.

Revenue Money received by a business as a result of sales.

Running costs (or operational costs) Those costs that arise out of the operation of the business.

Start-up costs Those costs paid once, when a business is first set up.

Chapter 19
Making a profit

IN THE NEWS

Joel Harrison is a sixth-form student at a large college in the North of England. As the son of a sheep farming family Joel had always thought of grass as being something of an asset. He knew that farmers actually had to pay for grazing if they could not rear sheep on their own land. This was an additional cost to many sheep farmers, including his father's farm. Joel knew that his father even had to rent fields from neighbouring landowners in order to be able to feed all of his flock. Working in the library at the college, Joel was disturbed one afternoon by the sound of heavy mowing equipment. He looked out of the library window to see two huge industrial mowing machines cutting the vast lawns of the college. He was immediately hit by a bright idea and contacted the college authorities.

Now Joel's father rents some of his sheep to the college. Sheep are good for lawns and they keep the lawns in good trim. On top of this, there is the added benefit of them providing a calming rural backdrop to the students' studies. Mr Harrison receives some rent from the college and, of course, gets to feed his sheep for free. The college saves money because it no longer has to hire noisy and expensive contractors. Students and staff can also see that it is getting closer to its environmental targets. Joel has made money out of the deal by acting as the 'middle man' between his father and the college. As a business, he is automatically a sole trader, as he has not chosen any other form of business (see Chapter 8). This means that not only does he get to keep any rewards, but he also carries all the risk and responsibility. He has looked at the possibility of providing the service to other organisations but needs first to know if he is making a profit.

His revenue comes from the college, which has paid him for setting up the service. However, he does not yet know if he is making a profit, as there are other costs involved. He has had to provide fencing, and has taken out insurance against any damage or nuisance that the sheep may cause. His father delivered the first flock, but he will be responsible for transport if he sells the service to other organisations. He also needs to include the costs of his own time taken to set up and manage the project.

Joel's unique business

@ The government's site for start-ups at **www.startups.co.uk/66788429117 18766542/making-a-profit.html** has a calculator for a business to see if it will make a profit. Input some costs for Joel (or a business of your choice) and see what sort of issues there might be.
On **www.mybusiness.co.uk/ YVM1eXBotKRAKg.html** you will find a long list of possible costs a business should include. See if you can think of any others.

Making a profit

> **Did you know...**
> Break even is often worked out on output. In other words, a business can say 'if we produce x amount, we will break even'. This is not accurate. Break even will only be reached if the business produces *and sells* the output.

Accounting and predictions

As with many small businesses, it is important that Joel looks to the future. It may be that he will make a loss in the first couple of years but is prepared to ride this out in order to make a profit once the business has built up. Businesses do not always make a profit in their first few months, or even years, of operation. Joel may have to borrow in order to cover his start-up costs and hope that future expansion will enable him to go into profit. He can only take this risk by 'looking into the future'. He has to use the figures and accounts that he has drawn up for the business and project what might happen in the future. Asking 'what if such-and-such happens' or 'what if such-and-such a cost rises' is called making 'what-if' predictions. Such predictions can only be made on the back of accurate accounts.

Target

Joel's first target is likely to be to break even. In other words, he needs to make enough revenue from selling his service to cover the costs of providing the service. If he was dealing with just one stream of revenue, and one set of costs, this would be easy. But, as with all businesses, there are various different costs to be taken into account.

Break even

Break even is the financial position where the total revenue of a business (the total amount of money coming into the business from sales and other activities) is equal to the total cost. At this point the business is making neither a profit nor a loss. It can be shown on a break even chart which shows costs against revenues and includes fixed costs, variable costs, total costs and sales revenue. (See table.)

Number sold	Sales revenue	Fixed cost	Variable cost	Total cost
0	0	15	0	15
1	10	15	5	20
2	20	15	10	25
3	30	15	15	30
4	40	15	20	35
5	50	15	25	40

> **Did you know...**
> The revenue of a business refers just to its income from sales. Businesses can make other income, for example, from investments, licence fees or franchise arrangements.

Profit and loss account

The profit and loss account shows what profit has been made, and where it has gone to. This is drawn up to show what has happened in the past (usually) six or twelve months of operation. It shows the past performance of the business. Here is a typical account for a small business, in this example a retailer called Rodney selling chocolate bars.

The first part of the account is called the 'trading' account. In this Rodney includes:

- Sales revenue to show the number of sales x price for the products sold in the period that the account covers. Rodney has sold 500 £1 bars.

- For any product that the business has sold, there will be an associated cost. For example, the raw materials or components used to make the product. For our retailer this is the price that he has paid for the chocolate bars. Rodney paid 50p each for the bars.

Trading Account

Sales revenue	500 × £1	500
Minus Cost of sales	opening stock 100 plus purchases 600 less closing stock 200 = 500 × 50p =	250
Gross profit		**250**

Profit and Loss Account

Gross profit	250
Minus Expenses	50
Net profit	**200**

- To know the cost of sales accurately, Rodney has to work out how much stock he actually bought in the period. Rodney has some stock at the start of the period (opening stock), bought more stock when he needed it (purchases) and has some stock left over (closing stock). The difference is the cost of the stock bought.

Gross profit shows the profit Rodney made on sales and is the first figure on the next part of the account, called the 'profit and loss' account.

Some of Rodney's stock

From this trading profit, Rodney takes the various other **expenses** that he has had to pay: rent for the shop, wages, electricity, petrol for his van, interest on loans, business rates, cleaning costs, telephone bills – in fact, all of the running costs (also called operating costs or **overheads**) of the business. In here, Rodney would also add in any other income of the business such as rent, interest on bank deposits or investment income. This gives him **net profit** for the period.

The third part of the account (called the 'appropriation' account, and not shown in our example) shows what happens to this profit. Some may go in taxation, some may be kept to reinvest, some may go to the owners.

Did you know...

Profit maximisation (the making of as much profit as possible) is often given as the central aim of businesses. Other aims, such as independence, or providing a service, may be more important and there are also not-for-profit business organisations such as charities (see Chapter 5).

Making a profit

Summary

- Profit is the reward for enterprise
- Profit is made when revenues are greater than costs
- When costs are greater than revenues the business is making a loss
- It is important to count in all costs
- Break even is when costs and revenues are equal
- A profit and loss account shows where money has come from, and where it has gone to

Core knowledge

What is profit? Profit is the reward for enterprise, or risk taking, and may be considered to be the main reason why many businesses are in business. Profit is defined as what is left once costs have been taken from revenue, as long as this is a positive figure. If costs are greater than revenue then this is a loss.

The important thing about calculating profit is to make sure that all costs have been taken into account. If this does not happen, then a false picture of profitability will emerge. Often, particularly in small or start-up businesses, the owner's own time is not costed in. In such cases it is easy to overestimate the amount of profit that has been made. Many small business owners and entrepreneurs are dedicated to their business, and put in long hours and a lot of hard work. This should be properly costed before deciding whether the business is worth operating. Against this, of course, go the benefits of working for yourself, setting your own hours and goals and reaping the rewards if the business is a success.

Profit is also a signal to other businesses that this is an area where they might be able to compete. If a business is making a profit in a market, then there is room for competition. If losses are being made, then this acts as a signal that one or more businesses should leave the market.

And more

The table earlier in this chapter shows the various elements in calculating break even. Building a break even graph from a chart is fairly straightforward. There are just four lines to consider. Fixed costs are those which do not alter as output alters, this is therefore shown on the graph as a horizontal line (FC). Variable costs are those that change as output changes and are therefore shown as rising as output rises (VC). Adding fixed costs to variable costs gives total costs (TC). Total revenue (TR) shows price x sales. The point where total cost is equal to total revenue is the break even point. To the left of this point, total costs are higher than total revenue, so the business is making a loss, to the right of this point, total costs are lower than total revenue, so the business is making a profit. The further away sales are from the break even point, the greater the profit or loss. Because there are so many different costs in most businesses, and of different types, it is not always easy to say which should be included and where, so it is often hard to be accurate about break even. This makes it a tool of limited use. It does, however, give clues as to the sort of methods that a business could use to reach or increase profit. Increasing price might increase revenue, lowering costs would enable break even to be reached earlier. Break even tables also show that fixed costs become less of an issue when spread over higher levels of output.

AQA BUSINESS FOR GCSE: SETTING UP A BUSINESS

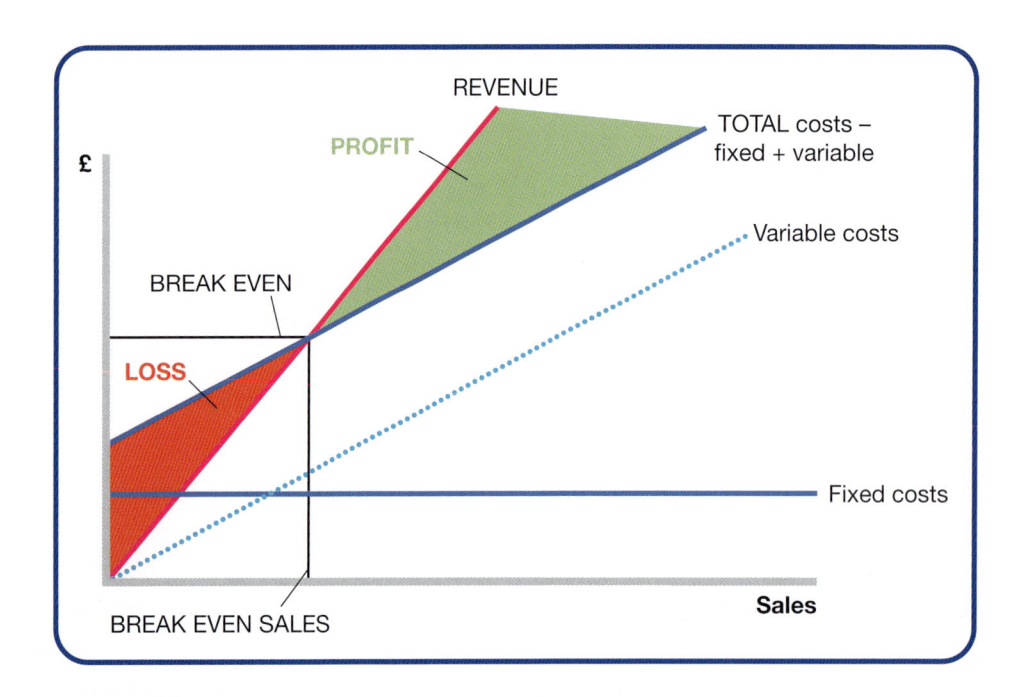

[Break-even chart showing Revenue, Total costs (fixed + variable), Variable costs, Fixed costs, Profit area, Loss area, Break even point and Break even sales on axes of £ against Sales]

Have a go

Group activity

Draw up a profit and loss account from the following figures for a small business selling widgets. Wendy's Widgets has bought and sold 400 boxes of small, 250 boxes of medium and 22 boxes of large widgets in the past six months. She buys widgets at £8 for a box of small, £9 for a box of medium and £12 for a box of large. Wendy sells widgets at £10 for a box of small or medium and £13 for a box of large. Her expenses in the period include rent £200, labour £400, transport £350, power £50, and insurance £25. Has Wendy made a profit?

Profit and Loss Account	TOTAL
Sales revenue	
Cost of sales	
Gross profit	
Expenses	
Transport	
Labour	
Rent	
Power	
Insurance	
Net profit (before tax)	

Discussion

Looking at the figures for Wendy's Widgets, do you think it is worth Wendy staying in business? What advice would you give her regarding her business?

Making a profit

Web-based activity

Explain why 'what-ifs' are important to a business. Show how you could make use of a spreadsheet to work out 'what ifs'.

Quickfire questions

1. Describe what is meant by a 'what if' in business.
2. Give an example of a typical 'what if'.
3. Define break even.
4. What is 'gross profit'?
5. What is 'net profit'?
6. Explain what is meant by 'cost of sales'.
7. What is the 'trading account'?
8. List the typical expenses of a small business.
9. What are 'overheads'?
10. Explain how profit acts as a signal to other businesses.

Hit the spot

- Describe how a break even point can be calculated.
- Explain how some businesses mistakenly calculate break even on output rather than sales. What problems is this likely to cause?
- Explain why profit is called the 'reward to enterprise'. What other rewards might be as important to the entrepreneur? Give reasons for your answer.

Cracking the code

Break even The point when costs equal revenues.

Expenses The costs to a business of all the services and other inputs used to run the business.

Gross profit Profit before expenses have been taken off.

Net profit Profit after expenses have been taken off.

Overheads Also called running costs: the day-to-day costs of operating the business.

Profit maximisation Making as much profit as possible.

Chapter 20
Managing cash flow

IN THE NEWS

Cash flow problems are likely with any small business, but especially with any business where cash comes in on an irregular basis. The Little Theatre, in Dale, is typical of many small community theatres which struggle to keep money coming through the doors all year round. Theatres find themselves in the position – as do all businesses – of having to pay fixed costs even when there is no performance. The Little Theatre has to pay its council tax and business rates, and standing charges to gas and electricity companies, whether or not it has a performance on. There are also some of its staff who are full time, as it is not possible (or desirable) to take on temporary staff for certain jobs. The caretaker, for example, needs to open the building in the morning, clean it and ensure that it is made secure and locked up at night. Even worse, its costs rise during a rehearsal period – staff and rooms are required and lighting and heating costs go up. Actors need to be paid once they are cast in a part and in rehearsal, props and costumes need to be bought or made and permissions to perform bought from the copyright holders of the play. All of this has to be paid before a single ticket is sold or even printed. (Ticket printing and publicity are even more costs that have to be paid before the doors open to the public.)

The Little Theatre's biggest money spinner is the annual Christmas pantomime. This starts its run in November and continues far into the New Year. In fact, it runs for as long as there is an audience coming to see it, and the theatre managers hope that, in most years, this will take them to the start of March. The pantomime does not always play to a full

Panto season

house, and eventually has to close as audiences dwindle. However, during its busiest four weeks, either side of Christmas Day, it is a sell-out, with both afternoon matinee and evening performances. Management has to try, each year, to take enough money in this period to support the theatre for the rest of the year. It also has to think of other ways to generate cash when the theatre is not staging a performance and to try to come up with ways of spreading or delaying payments to suppliers.

@
Go to **www.thisistheatre.com/panto.html**. What performances are on in your area? List the ways in which each theatre is trying to spread cash flow.
Visit **www.fireworks.co.uk**. How many ways of increasing firework sales can you find? Can you think of any other ways?

Managing cash flow

> **Did you know...**
> The more detailed the cash flow statement or forecast is, the easier it is for the business to recognise problem areas and do something about them. Many businesses therefore create very detailed cash flow charts.

Cash flow statement						
£	Month 1	Month 2	Month 3	Month 4	Month 5	Month 6
Balance brought forward	1000	–1000	–1000	–2000	2000	5000
Sales revenue	2000	2000	2000	4500	3500	4000
Cash in hand	3000	1000	1000	2500	5500	9000
Cash out	4000	2000	3000	500	500	1000
Balance carried forward	–1000	–1000	–2000	2000	5000	8000

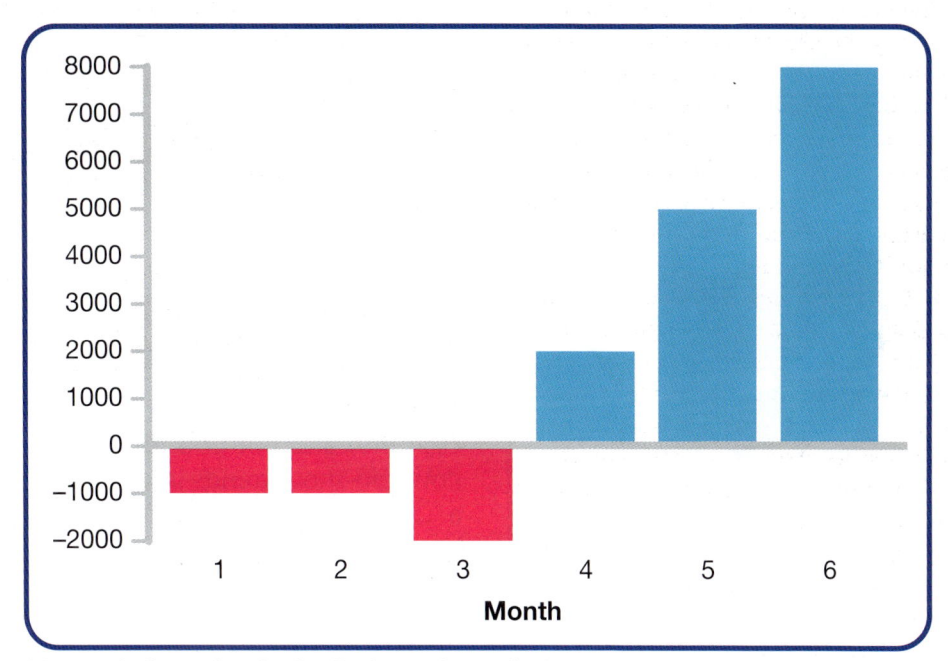

Net cash flow, that is the 'balance brought forward' line from the table

> **Did you know...**
> Terms in business finance have a very precise meaning and it is important that you understand them. Revenue, income and cash all refer to money. Can you define what each means in a business sense?

Cash flow

The Little Theatre can use the financial accounts that it has drawn up to see whether or not it is making a profit. This, however, shows it the position at the end of a period of time, rather than during it. It may be that, by the end of the year, the theatre is making a profit, but this does not show the full picture, or possible problems during the year. This is the case for many businesses that face uneven flows of cash into and out of their business. In the most extreme cases, for instance seasonal products, a business will have to make all its sales in a very short period and use this money to support itself for the rest of the time. Typical seasonal products include Christmas decorations, ice cream, fireworks, holidays and many different kinds of fruit and vegetable.

Seasonal sales of these products peak in December

Cash shortages

The Little Theatre needs to know when cash is going to come in and, just as importantly, when it needs to go out in terms of payments to suppliers and for services like **utilities**, marketing and communications. It is often a shortage of cash rather than a lack of orders that is the reason for the failure of a business. If a bill becomes due for payment, and the business does not have the cash to meet it, this can spell disaster. Imagine a delivery service that could not afford its fuel bill, or a retailer that does not have the money to pay the rent on the shop, or a farmer that doesn't have the money to pay for seed. In each case, even though the business may be a viable one – even a successful one – a lack of cash could see **creditors** forcing the business to close, so that they can be paid from the sale of its **assets**.

Cash flow table

A cash flow table shows the flows of money into and out of a business. Cash flow is often pictured as a bathtub, with cash flowing into it from the taps, and out again through the plughole. There are problems for the business if the tub overflows or runs dry! If it overflows, this means that the business has too much cash, which could be invested to make money. If it runs dry, then the business may not be able to pay its bills.

Cash flow forecast

A cash flow forecast shows predicted flows of cash into and out of a business. A detailed cash flow can show trends in costs and prices and be a useful management tool. It lets the business know when it will need to borrow money, how much it will need to borrow and for how long. This can help it not only to have financing in place, but to choose the most appropriate type of finance.

Managing cash flow

There are two ways for a business to manage cash flow. One is to increase revenue or, if this is not possible, to spread revenue, so that it comes in more evenly. The other is to reduce or spread costs. Many businesses that sell seasonal products will try to spread sales throughout the year, by making products popular at other times.

Managing cash flow 119

Solutions to cash flow problems

To spread revenue, the Little Theatre could sell advance tickets or season tickets to shows. This brings some revenue in ahead of actual ticket sales. It could also try to create new revenue streams. For example, the foyer space could be used for art exhibitions, or rented to another business as a coffee bar or café. It could try to bring its costs down or, if this is not possible, spread or reschedule payments. For example, it could pay utility bills monthly rather than in a lump sum.

In the UK, seasonal sales of these products peak in November

Did you know...

Firework manufacturers have successfully moved some firework sales in the UK away from the run-up to 5 November by promoting them for weddings and other events and celebrations.

Summary

- A business needs to control flows of cash
- Cash flows into and out of a business exist both when it starts up and when it is operating
- Cash flow problems are one of the main causes of business failure
- Businesses can help cash flow by increasing or spreading revenue
- Businesses can help cash flow by decreasing or spreading costs
- Cash flow forecasts are a powerful management tool

Core knowledge

The main cash inflows happen firstly when the business is set up, and then when it starts operating. The first inflows are the cash used to start the business, for example owners' funds, loans and grants (see Chapter 16). Once the business is operating, there are then inflows of sales revenue. The main outflows are also in two parts. When setting up, the business will need to buy stock, premises, machinery, tools, etc. and to pay for marketing and promotion. Once operating, the outflows continue – buying stock, paying interest on loans, taxation, expenses such as rent, rates, wages, power and communication charges. If there is more flowing into a business than leaving it the business has a cash **surplus**. If there is more flowing out than in, there is a cash **deficit**. A cash flow statement shows flows in and out of the business in the past. A forecast estimates what those flows will be in the future. It is a month by month prediction of how much cash will be needed, so that the business can plan ahead and make sure that:

- it has enough cash to cover payments when they become due;
- it does not carry too much cash.

Carrying too much cash is as much of a problem as not having enough. Money that is in tills, or current accounts, could be earning interest for the business if it was invested.

And more

There are two different types of accountant. Financial accountants look after and record the costs and revenues of a business: its income and expenditure. They also make sure that its accounts are accurate for the people who need them, such as the tax authorities and the owners.

Management accountants use the internal financial information of the business. These figures are only available to the managers and owners of the business. (Many of the figures used by financial accountants are, especially in limited companies, available to the public.) They are figures and accounts that are used to work out how well the business is doing and how to move it forward. They involve managers in making forecasts and in planning for the future. These accounts are vital in planning the future direction of the business and are the major tools in strategic planning. The major tools used are budgets (working out future spending and income) and ratios, which measure one factor in terms of another (for instance how productive a machine is in terms of its cost) to show efficiency or effectiveness and forecasts. A management accountant would not be interested in a cash flow statement, for example, but would want to know about the forecast future cash flows of the business so that this could be managed. Management accountants are often found in positions of power and responsibility in a business, and rise to top management positions.

Managing cash flow

Have a go

Group activity

Each person in your group should set up a spreadsheet to calculate cash flow for an imaginary business. Look at how other people have used formulae and decide on the most efficient way to set up the spreadsheet.

Discussion

If a sole trader cannot pay a bill, creditors can take him or her to court. If the court decides to make the person bankrupt, it can force the sale of his or her possessions in order to pay the bill.
Do you think that creditors – which are often big companies like electricity suppliers - should be allowed to do this?

Web-based activity

Find out all you can about company 'receivers'. What is their role? What link do you think they have with cash flow problems?

Quickfire questions

1. Describe one possible cash inflow when a business is at start-up stage.
2. Describe one possible cash outflow when a business is at start-up stage.
3. Describe one possible cash inflow when a business is at operational stage.
4. Describe one possible cash outflow when a business is at operational stage.
5. Give three examples of products that have seasonal sales.
6. What is a creditor?
7. What is an asset?
8. Describe how a cash shortage could be a problem for a business.
9. Describe how a cash surplus could be a problem for a business.
10. Give two possible ways to solve a cash flow problem.

Hit the spot

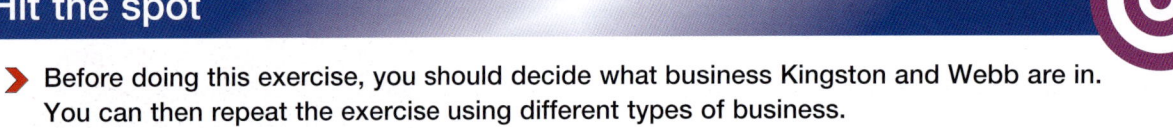

> Before doing this exercise, you should decide what business Kingston and Webb are in. You can then repeat the exercise using different types of business.

> Look at the six month cash flow forecast for Kingston and Webb (page 117). Suggest ways to improve the forecast.

> Identify the months when Kingston and Webb may have problems of cash shortages and suggest what they should do to solve the problems.

> What is the problem from months 4 to 6? Explain why this is a problem, and suggest possible solutions.

Cracking the code

Assets What the business owns, such as stock or equipment or vehicles.

Creditor Someone, or a business, that is owed money.

Deficit When cash outflows are greater than inflows.

Surplus When cash inflows are greater than outflows.

Utilities Services such as water, gas and electricity.

PEOPLE IN BUSINESSES

SECTION 5

Chapter 21
Recruiting staff

IN THE NEWS

Education Sense

Probably all school students know what a supply teacher is. It's the person who replaces the full-time teacher when he or she is off ill or on a training course. Sometimes these teachers are called cover or relief teachers. Schools will often hire a supply teacher by phoning up an agency. Karl Gannon runs one of these agencies, which he calls Education Sense. The agency is based in the south-east of England.

Karl seems the most unlikely person to start a teacher agency. He did not have a positive experience at school when he was young. Karl suffers from dyslexia, which made it difficult for him to progress at school. He was expelled when he was 13, and ran away from home when he was 14.

With no GCSE qualifications to his name, Karl found it difficult to find work. But with funding and support from the Prince's Trust, he managed to get his own business off the ground. Karl decided to specialise in providing special educational needs (SEN) teachers and teaching assistants. He felt that he had been let down when he was at school because his own needs had not been recognised. He was determined to improve things for students who had trouble learning.

Karl needs to recruit teachers regularly to have on his books. He advertises for them in newspapers, but he relies mostly on Education Sense's web pages to attract teachers to the agency.

Once a person has shown an interest in becoming a supply teacher, Karl will ask him or her to complete an **application form**. The form will ask the applicant to give details of their teaching experience and other information, such as whether the person wants full-time or part-time work. If Karl believes that the person applying is suitable, an **interview** will be held. Karl needs to check that the teacher has the right sort of personality and interests to work with SEN children. If it is necessary, Education Sense will provide training in working with special needs students.

The person applying will also be police checked. This means Education Sense will ask the police if there are any reasons why this person should not be allowed to work with children.

Karl believes that it is important to have a good working relationship with the schools that take his supply teachers. He will visit each one personally to find out about the school. Care will then be taken to make sure that the supply teacher that Karl sends to the school matches its needs.

Take a look at Karl's web page at:
www.education-sense.com

> **Did you know…**
> Part-time employees have the same rights as full-time staff. They can't, for instance, be paid at a lower rate or made redundant just because they are not full-time workers.

A job interview

> **Did you know…**
> Staff wages are often the highest cost a small business has to pay, particularly for those in the service sector.

Full-time and part-time employees

Education Sense encourages both part-time and full-time teachers to apply to the recruitment agency. Many employees prefer to work part-time. This could be because:

- They have family or other commitments that do not allow them to be away from home for long periods. When part-time work is offered, employers will find it easier to recruit students and mothers with young children.
- Employees might prefer two or three part-time jobs rather than have a full-time one. This can bring additional security, as if one job ends for some reason; there is another to provide income to the worker. Some people may also like the variety that several part-time jobs bring.

Recent laws have made it illegal to treat part-time employees any differently than their full-time co-workers. So, part-timers have the same job security. They cannot be made redundant before full-time workers are, just because they work part-time. Also, the same wage rate must be given to part-timers as is paid to full-time employees doing the same work.

Full-time employees can bring benefits to businesses:

- Full-timers are more likely to be up to date with what is going on in the business.
- They can become more skilful because they are using their skills more often.
- They know their co-workers better and can fit in more easily as part of a team.
- If the employees have direct contact with customers, then it helps to have full-timers. Customers like to deal with familiar faces.

> **Did you know…**
> The more loyal a business's employees are, the longer they are likely to remain. This means lower recruitment and training costs. But recent European research shows that 28.5 per cent of UK employees are actively looking for a new job.

AQA BUSINESS FOR GCSE: SETTING UP A BUSINESS

Summary

- Recruiting staff can be a complicated and time-consuming activity. It can also be expensive in terms of time and effort needed to get the right person for the job.
- It is important that small businesses in particular take care to recruit the right people. If you only employ three people and one is weak that is a large proportion of your staff.
- There are both benefits and disadvantages in employing part-time staff.

Core knowledge

Recruitment

Before an employee is recruited it would make sense to consider if the employee is actually needed. Employing somebody is a long-term commitment. When an employee leaves a business, the business owner could use this opportunity to consider whether the leaver actually needs to be replaced. Or, would it be better to recruit someone with different skills?

A large business might write a detailed job description and a person specification at this point. This way, the managers will have a much clearer idea of the type of person that they are looking for. It is unlikely that a small business will go to this trouble. But the owner of a small business must make sure that he or she recruits a suitable person. A poor choice of employee will have a much bigger impact on a small business than a large one.

It is for this reason that owners might want to promote someone from within the business to fill the vacancy. This is called internal **recruitment**. The owner of the business will know how well the person works. The promotion might even motivate the employee to work even harder. This would only be suitable, however, for recruiting a supervisor or manager. It also means that there will be a vacancy for the promoted person's previous job.

Businesses might choose to recruit from outside the business, which is known as external recruitment. There are different ways that they can attract suitable people:

- *Recruitment agency* These are businesses like Education Sense. They will specialise in providing suitable employees, saving the business the trouble of doing this themselves.
- *Jobcentres* These are government agencies that allow job seekers to find suitable work. The centre will also inform businesses of people on their books who might be suitable for the vacancy. Jobcentres do not charge businesses for their services.
- *Advertise the vacancy* If a business needs a new employee it is more likely to advertise the job to attract people to apply. Where it advertises will depend upon the business. A small business might advertise in a local newspaper.

A recruitment agency

Selection process

The **selection** process has specific stages:
- *Completing an application form* The application form allows the business to sort out those people who are suitable. Applicants who do not have the required skills or qualifications will be rejected.
- *Short listing* This is when unsuitable candidates are discounted, leaving a smaller, manageable number of people to be interviewed.
- *Interview* This might be a formal meeting with the applicant where the employer asks a series of questions. The employer is trying to determine if the person is capable of doing the job and is motivated. This meeting also gives the applicant a chance to find out about the job and the business.
- *Trial period* Sometimes employees are not taken on permanently until they have successfully completed a trial period. This means they will be watched closely for the first few months. If the work they do is not good enough, they could be asked to leave at the end of the trial period.

And more

The owner of the business might already have a good idea whom he or she wants to fill the vacancy. It could be a person who is working for a competitor. Attracting the employee would save on training as the person already has the skills needed. There is another benefit: a competitor could be losing a key member of staff. Also the former employee might bring along useful information about the competing business. This method of recruitment is sometimes called head hunting or poaching. Not all businesses see poaching as a fair method of recruiting staff.

Sometimes the owner of a small business will ask the people who work in the business if they know anybody suitable for the job vacancy. Recruiting this way is cheaper, as there is no need to pay for an advertisement. There is more chance that the person recommended would fit in to the business if he or she is already known by people employed there. This type of recruitment can also be a good thing as the person who recommended the new employee would not want that employee to do anything to let him or her down.

Have a go!

Group activity

Imagine your school or college needs a new bursar/finance officer, or similar position. As a team, complete the following:
- outline/description of the job;
- list of the skills and qualifications needed;
- newspaper advertisement;
- programme for the day of the interview;
- list of questions to be asked at interview.

Discussion

Discuss in groups whether full-time employees are more likely to be loyal to the business than part-timers.

Quickfire questions

1. What is an application form?
2. What is a employee recruitment agency?
3. What is meant by internal recruitment?
4. Give an advantage of recruiting internally.
5. Describe two methods Education Sense uses to make sure the right type of teacher is recruited.
6. Give two reasons why Education Sense prefers to recruit teachers using its web pages.
7. Produce a list of three questions that Karl Gannon might ask teachers when he interviews them? Explain why you have chosen each of these questions.
8. Give an argument both for and against using a trial period before an employee is taken on permanently.
9. Give a reason why many businesses prefer to get their staff from recruitment agencies.
10. Give an argument both for and against recruiting staff on the recommendation of a current employee.

Hit the spot

- What is meant by (i) recruitment; (ii) selection?
- Explain two reasons why employers sometimes prefer to appoint part-time staff.
- Discuss the arguments for and against promoting somebody already working in the business, rather than appointing a person from outside.

Cracking the code

Application form A document filled in by someone wanting to work for a business. The form asks for personal details, employment history and experience.

Interview A chance for the employer and the applicant to meet. It can be formal, with the applicant being asked a series of questions, or just a chat.

Recruitment The process of an employer finding people who might be suitable to employ.

Selection The process of choosing the right person for the job.

Chapter 22
Rewarding staff

IN THE NEWS

Country Estates Garden (CEG) Furniture

CEG Furniture manufactures high quality garden furniture using traditional British timbers of elm and oak. The business is based in the Midlands, but sells its products all around the country. The furniture is targeted at the upper end of the market with prices much higher than customers would expect to pay for lower quality products at garden centres. The business sells through the internet and magazines like *Worcestershire Life*. There is also a display area outside the factory, where customers can inspect the furniture.

CEG employs five woodworkers who produce the furniture using traditional skills. There is also a part-time driver and a part-time secretary. A manager oversees the running of the company. The business is known for its friendly working environment. All but one of the employees have been there for at least ten years.

Each of the woodworkers is paid a **basic wage** of about £320 per week for a 40-hour week. If these workers are asked to work **overtime** because a large order has been received, 'time and a half' is given for hours above eight hours a day. The business's manager, John, is paid a salary of about £30,000 a year. He does not receive any overtime payments, and often works more than ten hours each day.

Besides the wage it pays to its woodworkers, CEG allocates 2 per cent of its profits to share between all employees according to how long they have worked there. Profits last year were £280,000. All employees are allowed to buy the furniture at a big **discount**, but even at the lower price, it is too expensive for them. At Christmas CEG gives each of its employees a luxury hamper.

Did you know...

In 2007, you had to earn £906 per week to be in the top 10 per cent of earners in the UK. If you earned less than £252, you were in the bottom 10 per cent.

AQA BUSINESS FOR GCSE: SETTING UP A BUSINESS

> **Did you know...**
>
> The occupations with the highest earnings in 2007 were 'health professionals' with £1019 a week, followed by 'corporate managers' (£702) and 'science and technology professionals' (£670). The lowest paid of all full-time employees were 'sales occupations', at £264 a week.
>
> National Statistics, 2008

Types of reward

CEG rewards its staff in several ways. These rewards can be split into two types: monetary and non-monetary. Most of the monetary rewards come from the wages that are paid each week. The annual **bonus** is another form of monetary reward. Employees, however, will only receive this payment if the business makes a profit, and if they have been there for long enough. Some of the longer-established employees would get a much bigger payment than those who only just qualify for it. This could cause some resentment, particularly if people feel that they have all worked equally hard to make the business profitable.

It is common practice for employers to pay workers at a higher hourly rate when they work longer than their **contracted hours**. Overtime rates vary though from business to business. CEG is quite generous in paying 1.5 times the normal hourly rate. Some businesses pay the lower rate of 'time and a quarter' or 1.25 times the normal hourly rate.

The non-monetary rewards include the Christmas hamper. This could be seen as a fringe benefit for working for CEG. There are other such benefits, however. The discount on the furniture could be viewed as another benefit. It could be argued that, because nobody takes up the offer to buy the furniture, it is not a genuine reward to the staff.

There are aspects of the job that could be seen as being a non-monetary reward. The case study says that the business is known for its friendly working environment. If CEG employees enjoy this, then in a sense they are being rewarded. Imagine one of the employees being offered an extra £30 per week to go and work for another business that was not as friendly a place. If he decided not to take up the offer, then in a way he has decided that the friendly environment at CEG is worth at least £30 to him.

The Christmas hamper is a non-monetary reward for employees

> **Did you know...**
>
> In 2008, the head of Virgin Atlantic, Richard Branson, admitted in a letter to his workforce that they could earn more working for another airline. He recognised though that many employees have fun and get job satisfaction working for Virgin.

Rewarding staff 131

Summary

- Workers are rewarded in more ways than just wages or salaries
- Rewards can be classed as monetary or non-monetary
- If a person enjoys a job, he or she might be not be prepared to move, even for a higher wage

Core knowledge

Wages and salaries

People often confuse these two terms. They both refer to financial rewards for working for a business, but the methods are different. Wages are usually paid either weekly or fortnightly, while salaries are paid monthly. However, the main difference is that wages are paid for undertaking so many hours work, but salaries are paid for doing a particular job. A manager will be paid a salary for managing a business. He will be expected to put in all the hours necessary to do the job, and not be able to claim overtime payments.

In the case study it says that John, the manager, often worked ten hours each day. Clearly, John felt that the job needed this amount of time to get the work done. The woodworkers on the other hand get paid more if they need to work more than eight hours each day.

Factors affecting the wages/salaries paid

The amount a person is paid, either as a salary or a wage, will depend on many factors. The law says that an employee must be paid at least the national minimum wage. This is considered in more detail in Chapter 24. The owner of a small business would probably look at the wages that are offered for similar jobs in other businesses when deciding on how much to pay his employees. Nevertheless, a worker may be offered a higher wage if he or she has more experience than others on lower wages, or has a particular skill that the business wants.

Fringe benefits are a common way of rewarding staff. Fringe benefits are rewards in addition to a person's normal wages or salaries. These are frequently used to motivate employees. More on this topic can be found in the next chapter.

A limited liability business might decide to offer employees shares in the company. These might be given freely or offered at reduced price. Many people believe that rewarding employees in this way will encourage them to work hard. If the business is successful this way, shareholders will receive a higher dividend. Another fringe benefit is helping the employee save for a pension. If the employee agrees, each week or month an amount of money is taken from his or her wages to put towards the pension. The employer will pay an additional amount to increase the saving (or contribution). Occasionally employers pay all of the pension contributions themselves, which is known as a non-contributory pension.

> ### And more
>
> There are other factors that influence just how much an employee earns. A business might use performance-related pay. This means the wage the employee gets paid depends upon the amount that is produced. At one extreme is **piecework**. With this system of payment an employee is paid so much for each item produced. Someone working in a factory assembling a circuit board may be paid 35p for each board made. If 20 can be made in an hour, the employee would be paid £7. Other performance-related systems might include a bonus payment for reaching a certain target. The problem with performance-related pay is that it is often difficult to measure the performance of a particular employee, especially when people work in teams. Also some jobs do not have any output to measure. How would you measure the output of a police officer, for example?
>
> In the case study for this chapter we looked at how someone might not be willing to move to another job, even if the financial rewards are higher. Many people take more than money into account when they consider the rewards that they receive for doing a job. You will be able to read more about this in the next chapter.
>
> If people enjoy the work that they do, we say they receive job satisfaction. In the example in the case study, the woodworker was not prepared to change jobs, even if he was offered an extra £30 per week. We could argue that the job satisfaction that he receives at CEG is worth £30 to him. If a business can improve the job satisfaction that its employees get, it will find it easy to retain them and still pay them lower wages that they could get elsewhere.

Have a go

Group activity

Working in a group, produce a PowerPoint presentation, or a podcast, explaining the different ways a small business might try to increase the job satisfaction that its employees receive.

Conduct a survey of people to determine the types of fringe benefits that they receive. The results should be presented as a series of graphs with sufficient explanation on a PowerPoint loop.

Quickfire questions

1. What is a fringe benefit?
2. What is piecework?
3. Give an example of a non-monetary reward.
4. Calculate the hourly rate of pay of the CEG woodworkers.
5. What is meant by CEG's customers being at the 'upper end of the market'?
6. Explain the difference between a wage and a salary.
7. What is meant by a non-contributory pension?
8. Explain why some employers allow employees to buy shares in the business at a discounted rate.
9. Explain a problem a business might have using performance-related pay.
10. Explain two possible reasons why one person is paid more than another.

Hit the spot

- What is meant by a non-monetary reward?
- Explain how a business could benefit by giving its employees non-monetary rewards.
- Discuss whether businesses need to offer similar wages as other businesses in order to retain their staff.

Cracking the code

Basic wage The wage paid for working the normal (contracted) hours.

Bonus An additional payment that usually has to be earned in some way or another.

Contracted hours The hours worked as stated in the contract of employment.

Discount A reduction in price.

Overtime Work done in excess of contracted hours.

Piecework A system of pay where someone is paid for how much is produced.

Chapter 23
Motivating employees

IN THE NEWS

Richer Sounds

Richer Sounds is a group of hi-fi stores that can be found around the UK. Julian Richer started the business when he was 19 years old. Julian believes that having a well-motivated staff has played an important part in the success of the business. It has been voted as one of the best places in Britain to work.

Enjoying yourself at work is seen as one way of getting the best out of employees. You need only step into Richer Sounds' head office in south-east London to realise that making work fun is a concept that Richer Sounds takes very seriously. Among the desks and computers you can find a whole army of wacky artworks, including a life-size Elvis. There is no stuffy dress code either. Jeans and t-shirts with shorts in the summer are encouraged to make employees feel comfortable. In a survey at Richer Sounds, 90 per cent of employees find their teams 'fun to work with', and 91 per cent say that they can have a laugh with co-workers.

Communication is seen as important within the organisation. All staff members are encouraged to voice their opinions if they are unhappy with any aspect of their work. There are also opportunities to give feedback at seminars, suggestion meetings and branch dinners. Richer Sounds operates a **suggestion scheme** for employees, with a cash bonus of at least £5 for each idea. This scheme has been remarkably successful, producing on average 20 suggestions a year from each employee.

The boss, Julian, has an open door policy. He is willing to speak to any employee if they have something to say. Salaries are high for the retail industry: a senior sales assistant can expect £18,000. The **perks** are also impressive: the loan of holiday homes in locations such as St Tropez and Venice; free massages, facials and pedicures at Christmas. There is even a take-your-pet-to-work scheme.

Employees at Richer Sounds have fun and are highly motivated

Promotion from within the business is normal. Most of the head office staff have worked on the shop floor. Richer Sounds claims that it is willing to recognise people's potential, and wants to allow them to develop within the business. For example, Lol Lecanu, the company's marketing director, started his career at Richer Sounds as a summer job on the shop floor.

Richer Sounds is also socially responsible, giving one of the highest proportions of pre-tax profits (5 per cent) to charity of any UK company. It is not surprising that 86 per cent of their employees say they are proud to work there.

Richer Sounds operates by these basic rules:

- *Rewards* If you want your staff to give great service, reward them for it.
- *Fun* On top of pay, provide extras that make the job enjoyable.
- *Communication* You can't motivate if you don't communicate.
- *Recognition* The best motivational technique is to say, 'Well done and thank you'.
- *Loyalty* If you want loyalty from people, you must give it to them.

Take a look at the Richer Sounds website:
www.richersounds.com

Motivating employees 135

> **Did you know...**
> The big dispute in motivation theory is whether wages are the most important factor in motivating employees.

There can be no doubt that Julian Richer has a different way of looking at how a business is run. He recognises the importance of having well-motivated employees. But he also knows that there has to be some control over his employees. What he says is: 'Little control and lots of motivation equals anarchy; lots of control and no motivation means repression.'

What managers need to do, according to Julian, is strike a balance between having very keen employees and making sure they are doing what you want them to do. It would be no good, for instance, to have sales staff being overfriendly with customers and bothering them, if they just wanted to browse at the products. Customers might see the sales assistants as being too pushy and be reluctant to come into the shops.

Julian Richer also recognises that it's not just money that motivates people. Many of the staff at Richer Sounds are young and respond well to a fun environment. Rewards can be equally fun and unpredictable. There might be prizes such as an evening's paintballing, hot air ballooning, or a weekend in Prague for the branch with the best sales.

The business wants to feel that its employees are enthusiastic about coming into work each day. Keen employees are more likely to treat customers well, and happy customers are more likely to spend money.

An unusual form of non-monetary reward

> **Did you know...**
> Many people give up their spare time to volunteer for unpaid work at charities, hospitals, and helping young people with sports, Duke of Edinburgh awards and organisations like the scouts. They are clearly not motivated by money.

Summary

- Richer Sounds is a business that recognises the important part its employees play in the success of its business
- Staff need to be motivated in order to give their best
- Money is not the only thing that motivates employees

Core knowledge

Over the years, businesses have developed a range of strategies to increase employee motivation. There has also been much research into this topic by universities and other organisations. There is no clear agreement about what is the best way to motivate people. Many people think that what motivates an employee depends upon the type of person and his or her personal circumstances.

Someone who needs money to bring up a family, might be motivated purely by wages. The more this worker is paid, the more enthusiastic he will be to do the work. Employees in their 50s and 60s may be looking for something quite different to motivate them. Money is possibly less important to this group of people. They might work better when they are in teams, enjoying the social side of working life, or like having the status of an important job.

Employees can also be motivated by the 'extras' that an employer provides. These are called fringe benefits and were discussed in the previous chapter.

There are other factors that influence just how happy an employee is. Nobody wants to think that their views are not important or are ignored by their boss. People also like to know what is happening in the business, particularly if there are to be changes. Having good communications between management and employees is usually seen to be a problem for larger organisations. This is because there are often different layers of management and, as a result, more levels for messages to go through before they get to every person. Communications are usually less of a problem within a small business because the employees probably see the manager on a regular basis.

Different employees have different motivations

> **And more**
>
> Work can become boring and monotonous if employees are performing the same task over and over each day. When this happens, employees can become sloppy and mistakes are made. Employers can help reduce the level of boredom by making employees' jobs more interesting, or giving employees the chance to move around from one job to another. For instance, someone who spends his working day cutting up identical pieces of wood may quickly become bored. The job can be made a little more interesting by giving the employee a range of lengths of wood to cut.
>
> A study of motivation many years ago concluded that workers needed to have all their basic requirements satisfied before they can be motivated. These requirements were called **hygiene factors** and included: safe and comfortable working conditions, suitable rest facilities and a decent wage.

Have a go!

Activity

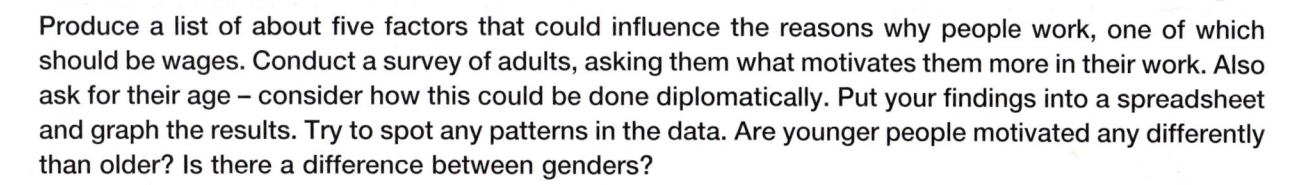

Produce a list of about five factors that could influence the reasons why people work, one of which should be wages. Conduct a survey of adults, asking them what motivates them more in their work. Also ask for their age – consider how this could be done diplomatically. Put your findings into a spreadsheet and graph the results. Try to spot any patterns in the data. Are younger people motivated any differently than older? Is there a difference between genders?

Quickfire questions

1. What type of business is Richer Sounds?
2. Give a way in which a shop assistant's job in a supermarket can be made more interesting.
3. What is an open door management policy?
4. Give two examples of how Julian Richer uses fun to liven up the workplace.
5. What is meant by hygiene factors?
6. Explain why the factors that motivate an 18 year old might be different from those that motivate a middle-aged person.
7. Give two reasons why Richer Sounds offers £5 for each suggestion given by its employees.
8. How are Richer Sounds employees able to get their views across to the management?
9. How does recruiting for managers within a business help with motivation?
10. Explain why Julian Richer believes that motivated staff still need some control.

Hit the spot

> Describe what is meant by motivation.

> Explain two benefits that a well-motivated workforce can bring to a business.

> Discuss whether a pay rise or improved working conditions is likely to have the bigger effect on employees' motivation?

Cracking the code

Hygiene factors The basic needs of an employee, including a reasonable wage.

Loyalty The willingness of an employee to remain at a business. Loyalty can also apply to supporting the business by not being late, taking unnecessary time off and talking positively about it.

Perk Another term to describe a fringe benefit, which is a reward to an employee in addition to his or her wages.

Suggestion scheme A system where employees give ideas to managers about how things can be improved in the business.

Chapter 24
Staff and the law

IN THE NEWS

The King's Head is a country pub and restaurant. Karen Tay, the new manageress, was taking over soon and decided to check that the business was complying with all the necessary **employment laws**. The previous manager, Stan, showed her around the business.

Stan started by saying that the gardener, who had been off ill for a week with a bad cold, was almost 65 years old. Stan explained that his birthday would be an ideal time to get him to retire and get someone younger in to do the work,

Karen also found that the two part-time waitresses were being paid the **minimum wage**, while the full-time waiter was on more than a pound an hour more than them. The previous owner had said that Karen might want to lower the wages of the waiting staff, as customers were generally good tippers, so they received money this way. He explained that he paid the full-time waiter more because he was a good worker and he didn't want to lose him.

Stan explained that he hadn't bothered to adapt any equipment in the pub because no disabled people worked there. He explained that it would be far too expensive to put in a ramp to allow a wheelchair to come through the door, so the pub wouldn't be able to take on anyone requiring such access.

When Karen asked whether any of the staff were pregnant, Stan laughed. He suggested that it would be dangerous for a pregnant woman to work in a pub, so she would have no real choice but to leave. Karen thought better about asking about the arrangements for paternity leave.

Employment laws apply to every workplace

AQA BUSINESS FOR GCSE: SETTING UP A BUSINESS

> **Did you know...**
> Before the Equal Pay Act of 1970, women were often paid less than men for doing exactly the same work. As recently as 2008, however, women on average earned 12.6 per cent less than men.

Employment laws

Clearly the King's Head is a fictitious case study. No business would be allowed to operate this way. Small businesses need to comply with the law as far as their employees are concerned. There are several examples in the case study when employment laws have been broken. The law says that businesses are not allowed to discriminate on the grounds of age, race, gender, sexuality, religion or disability. These laws usually apply no matter how large or how small the business is.

Age discrimination

The Age Discrimination Act came into force on 1 October 2006. It made it illegal for employers to discriminate on the grounds of a person's age. In the act of parliament, age means both old and young, unlike in some countries where it is just the old that are protected. It is illegal to pass over an applicant for employment or training just because of his age. There is no law that a person must leave when he or she reaches normal retirement age. This means it might be difficult to make the gardener retire at age 65 if he wishes to continue to work at the King's Head.

Disability discrimination

On 1 October 2004, the final part of the Disability Discrimination Act came into force. Part III specifies that all service providers, businesses and public sector services must take reasonable action to ensure disabled people can make full use of them. So, the King's Head is breaking the law by not providing suitable access for disabled people.

Is the workplace safe?

Providing access for people with disabilities

Staff and the law

Part-time workers

A law passed in 2000 made it illegal to treat part-time workers less favourably than their full-time equivalents. This means that they should receive the same hourly wage as their full-time co-workers. Similarly, they don't have to be the first choice to go, if a business finds that it has too many employees. The two part-time waitresses would have a strong case to be paid the same hourly wages as the full-time waiter. It would seem from the case study that they all do similar work.

Maternity leave/paternity leave

Maternity leave is a right by law to any woman. Women are allowed to take up to one year off work to have a baby. The mother is entitled to return to her previous job and not have to accept a demoted position. A business cannot dismiss a woman just because she is pregnant, or has a family to look after. Paternity leave is an entitlement for fathers of new babies.

An employee cannot be dismissed because she is pregnant

Did you know...

Other forms of discrimination are recognised by some people, but not yet put into laws. These include: adultism – giving preference to adults, such as no-children holidays; lookism – discriminating against someone because a person's appearance; and heightism – favouring tall people.

Summary

- There are many laws that protect employees
- A business is not allowed to discriminate on the grounds of age, race, gender, sexuality, religion or disability

AQA BUSINESS FOR GCSE: SETTING UP A BUSINESS

Core knowledge

When the owner of a new business decides to employ somebody, he or she must recognise that there are many laws that need to be considered. The employer cannot pick and choose which laws are obeyed, or think that the law doesn't apply to him or her.

Laws are changing all the time, and it is the responsibility of the employer to keep up to date with them. For instance, at the moment parents who have children under six have the right to apply to work flexibly. This means employers have to look into changing working hours, so mothers and fathers can spend more time with their children. This could be moving from full- to part-time working or changing the hours worked. Parents might, for example, want to be able to take their children to school and pick them up. Employers are required by law to consider these requests seriously. However, employees have no automatic right to demand flexible hours. This may change in the future though, so employees must keep up to date with the law.

It is sometimes said that when laws like this are passed, small businesses will find a way around them. They might argue that it is much easier to make arrangements for maternity leave in a large business with many employees. A key worker in a small business would have a much bigger impact if the business only employed five people. If a business puts undue pressure on an employee to quit, or refuses to employ anyone who might require maternity leave in the future, it would be breaking the law.

Businesses are also required to ensure that the workplace is safe for employees. An organisation called the Health and Safety Executive (HSE) regulates and enforces the rules about safety at work. These are set out in the Health and Safety at Work Act, 1974. This law says that it is the duty of businesses to make sure that employees operate in a safe environment. This is sometimes described as making sure that workers are able to return home as healthy as when they arrive at work.

And more

The need for laws to protect employees' rights can be blamed partly on some myths and prejudices in society. Older workers are sometimes thought of as being slow, forgetful and not willing to learn new skills. Young people, on the other hand, are regarded as lacking communication and interpersonal skills and not having commonsense. Obviously, these are generalisations, but still thought of as being true by a number of people. Some companies are now recognising that there are benefits in employing older workers. This is particularly relevant as there is a growing skills shortage in the UK.

It is for reasons like this that businesses cannot afford to overlook certain people when they are recruiting new employees. By making it difficult for disabled, elderly people and young women, who might become pregnant, to get a job, a business is reducing the number of talented people available to it.

There are a growing number of businesses that actively seek out groups of workers who have been discriminated against. Some of these set employment quotas or targets. This means businesses encourage discriminated groups to apply for jobs with them. This process is sometimes called **positive discrimination**.

Anyone who feels that he or she has been discriminated against in the workplace can take the case to an **Industrial Tribunal**. This is a type of court that deals with employment matters.

Staff and the law

Have a go!

Activity

Using ICT facilities, produce a leaflet on employment laws. This can take the form of an outline of the main features of the law, or a series of frequently asked questions (FAQs). The leaflet is intended to provide small businesses with basic information.

Quickfire questions

1. Which employment law was passed in 2004?
2. The Age Discrimination Act protects older workers only. True or false?
3. Describe the rights that a part-time worker has.
4. How long can a woman take for maternity leave?
5. What is paternity leave?
6. What is meant by health and safety regulations?
7. Explain two ways in which an elderly person might be discriminated against in the workplace.
8. Explain two problems that a business might have offering parents flexible working hours.
9. Explain two reasons why a worker might take his employer to an Industrial Tribunal.
10. Explain two ways a restaurant might need to adapt its premises to allow access to disabled people.

Hit the spot

- What is meant by discrimination in employment?
- If an employer has too many workers, describe a legal way she might decide whom to make redundant.
- Discuss whether it is necessary to have laws to protect employees.

Cracking the code

Employment law A series of laws designed to ensure that employees' rights are looked after and to protect them from being exploited by businesses.

Minimum wage The lowest hourly rate that a business can pay employees. The rate for young people is different to the one for adults.

Positive discrimination Being seen to make an effort to recruit or promote people from groups which have been discriminated against.

Industrial Tribunal A court that deals with employment issues, such as discrimination.

Chapter 25
Other legal responsibilities of business

IN THE NEWS

Going to a small claims court

Davies Builders is a small business that specialises in refitting kitchens and bathrooms in the Worcestershire area. Cash flow is always a problem for a business like Davies. The owner David needs to buy from a **supplier** the units and appliances that he needs to fit. He knows that he won't be paid until the bathroom or kitchen has been completed to the client's satisfaction. The suppliers will, however, want their money at the end of each month. Like many businesses in this position, Davies Builders' bank account is usually **overdrawn** until customers' bills are settled.

David was pleased to receive a new order for a bathroom, which came from the recommendation of a previous customer. The new client was keen to have the job done as quickly as possible. The **quote** of £4500 was accepted. David set about the job, completing it in a week. The customer appeared happy with her bathroom, so David sent out his **invoice** for the amount and waited. After two weeks of hearing nothing, he phoned to remind about the bill and was told the money would be there in a day or two. A week later it still hadn't arrived. He sent a reminder and waited again. Telephone calls went unanswered. A third letter was sent, but this time it threatened legal action.

During this time, the bathroom supplier was due to be paid the £2000 for the bathroom fittings. David had reached the limit of his overdraft and was struggling to pay his account. He had a good relationship with the supplier that he didn't want to spoil by not paying on time. Though he had never done it before, David realised that he would have to take the customer to the small claims court to recover his money.

The small claims court

@ Go to **www.businesslink.gov.uk** and search for information on how to take a customer to the small claims court.

Other legal responsibilities of business

> **Did you know…**
> According to the Debtline organisation, the UK has one of the worst paying business cultures in the EU.

Insurance

Small businesses are required to have proper insurance. Any vehicle the business owns must be insured. Employer's liability insurance is also compulsory by law for anyone operating in the UK and employing staff. This insurance protects the employee against acts of negligence. For instance, if an employee had an accident at work, or a customer was hurt in a shop. Businesses might choose to take out insurance to cover loss of earnings. If there was a fire, for example, this might mean the business cannot operate and loses money. Products insurance can be bought that protects a manufacturer in case there is a fault with the items it makes and a customer is injured. Professionals, such as doctors and lawyers can take out professional indemnity insurance in case mistakes are made and a client decided to sue the business.

Taxes

All small business traders need to keep records of their income and expenditure. Self-employed people need to put in annual tax returns, so the **HM Revenue & Customs** can work out how much tax they need to pay.

VAT (value added tax)

If a small business is registered for VAT purposes, it must charge its customers this tax for any goods that are liable to value added tax. The difference between what the business receives and what it has paid out in VAT on supplies is then sent to the government.

Recovering money through small claims courts

Small claims courts provide an easy, speedy and low-cost way for creditors to recover their money. Unlike the County Court, where it can be expensive because a barrister may be needed, small claims courts are much cheaper. A fee is

> **Did you know...**
> It has been estimated that nearly one third of the UK's business start-ups are operating without any business insurance.

charged by the court, which must be paid upfront. It costs £30 to recover a debt of up to £300. The fee rises to £120 for debts between £1000 and £5000. The maximum that can be claimed in these courts is £5000.

The system works well for small businesses. The cost of the fee for presenting the case at court is added to the amount the debtor owes. So in David's case, if he were successful he would receive £4620 from his customer: £4500 for the bathroom and his £120 court fee.

In this case study, David was suing a customer. He could equally have taken a business to court. When this happens, if the court case is successful, the business that was at fault will get a black mark against its name. This means that the business will have a poor credit history. When the business tries to obtain credit facilities in the future, such as getting a loan to buy a van, banks and other lenders will be reluctant to give it money.

Because of the threat of a poor record, **debtors** will often pay up and not risk contesting in court, even though they may feel that they have a case. There is always the risk that the judgment at a small claims court will go against the person claiming, which does put some people off using the court. An additional risk is that the debtor may not have the money to pay, even if the case goes against him. So, time and effort has gone into preparing for court, the fee paid and in the end no money is forthcoming.

Bad debts can make running a business difficult

> **Did you know...**
> Around 2 million small claims are made each year, and only a tiny proportion of those claims ever come to court – in many cases the threat of small claims does the trick, and payment follows quickly.

Summary

- Businesses have both moral and legal responsibilities to pay their debts
- Small businesses can use small claim courts to recover outstanding debts
- Many cases are settled before they go to court, as businesses do not want a judgment against them affecting their credit record

Other legal responsibilities of business

Core knowledge

Some would argue that bad debts are a way of life for small businesses. Every so often a non-payer will appear and you have to live with it. Many believe that it's simply easier to **write off** the debt than to go to the expense and inconvenience of recovering the money legally. It was to avoid this that the small claims courts were set up. As part of the County Court system, small claims courts can help traders such as David Davies fight back and recover outstanding debts.

Some of the legal issues to do with employing people can be found in Chapter 24. There are other legal issues that a business must address.

And more

Unpaid debts have a crippling effect on small businesses and the problem appears to be getting worse. Unpaid debts increase rapidly when the economy is slowing down because of a **recession**. Businesses have a **liquidity** problem. They do not have the cash to pay their debts so hold back as long as possible. This in turn means that **creditors** find it difficult to pay their own debtors. The overall effect is a downward spiral.

Small businesses will often have a more difficult time than larger companies when the payment of debts is concerned. Large companies are in a stronger position to negotiate delays in payments. A creditor would not want to lose the account of a large buyer, if the business decided to go elsewhere. So, suppliers will often push the small businesses first for payment, knowing that if they do not return, it is not a huge loss.

Recently the law was changed to allow creditors to charge debtors interest on any debts that were not paid by the agreed time. Not all small businesses enforce this law, however. They don't want to upset their customers, so they buy goods elsewhere in the future.

Have a go!

Activity

Imagine David Davies has asked you to help him prepare to take his case to the small claims court. Produce a written statement for him to present to the court.

Web-based activity

Use information from the Citizens' Advice Bureaux website **www.adviceguide.org** to produce a flowchart of the different stages that you should go through with small claims before getting to court.

Quickfire questions

1. What is a small claims court?
2. What is the maximum amount that can be recovered in a small claims court?
3. How much fee would someone have to pay at the small claims court fee to recover £2000?
4. What is an annual tax return?
5. By law, what type of insurance must all businesses have?
6. Explain why the number of claims for unpaid invoices increase during a recession.
7. Explain how a dentist might need professional indemnity insurance.
8. Explain why many small claims never actually reach the court hearing.
9. Why do small businesses often choose not to charge interest on outstanding debts?

Hit the spot

> Describe a problem a business might face if it did not have proper insurance.
> Explain why businesses do not always pay their debts.
>> Discuss whether a business should always try to recover money it is owed.

Cracking the code

Cash flow The overall effect of cash coming into and out of a business. If more money flows in to the business than out, it is called a positive cash flow.

Creditor Somebody who is owed money by another person or business.

Debtor A person or business that owes money to another.

HM Revenue & Customs The government body that collects taxes.

Invoice Another term for a bill. A formal request for money to be paid.

Liquidity A measure of how easily a business can pay off its immediate debts from cash it has or will receive shortly.

Overdrawn When more money has been spent than was in the bank account, which means the account holder is in debt to the bank.

Quote The amount of money a business is prepared to undertake a job for.

Recession A slowdown in the economy that happens every few years. Businesses do not sell as much, profits fall and workers are made redundant.

Supplier A business that sells materials to another business.

Write off To give up on the chances of recovering a debt.

SECTION 6
OPERATIONS MANAGEMENT

Chapter 26
Producing a good

IN THE NEWS

Farmhouse Fare

Helen Colley, the founder of Farmhouse Fare, was raised on a farm in rural Lancashire. Helen started a catering business at the age of 18 with £250 that she had borrowed. Over a 20-year period, Helen developed her business so that it became one of the largest outside caterers in Lancashire, specialising in providing food for large events that were often held in marquees.

Farmhouse Fare, a **manufacturer** of traditional puddings, only came about after Helen felt the need to **diversify** away from outside catering. Helen knew that the sticky toffee puddings she made were always popular with diners. She decided that she could sell the puddings during the cold winter when there was no marquee work available. By doing this, she could receive a regular cash flow and keep her full-time staff employed.

The year 2001 was an important one for farms in Britain. The outbreak of foot and mouth disease meant that outdoor catering dried up for Helen. Marqueed events were forbidden for fear of spreading the disease. Helen decided the time was right to make a full-time business based on her puddings.

Helen bought some large-scale containers and a mixer, so she could make larger quantities of puddings than she had before. Initially she sold her puddings through local stores and delicatessens. Her big breakthrough came when Sainsbury's agreed to stock her products. Now most of the major supermarkets buy puddings from her.

When producing the puddings, Helen works to the same basic recipe, but will adapt the style of pudding to meet the needs of the different type of customers that shop at each supermarket. The supermarket buyers give Helen guidance in what type of puddings their customers would enjoy.

As the business grew Helen found that she needed to move to larger premises. She now operates from a purpose-built unit a few miles down the road from her farm. Despite manufacturing the puddings from a **factory**, Helen keeps to the handcrafted nature of the puddings, which come in 14 different flavours. She is always willing to try a new idea for a pudding.

Helen insists on only using natural ingredients and producing the puddings in **batch** size quantities. She chooses not to use mass production methods. The puddings are still made traditionally by hand.

Take a look at Helen's website at
www.farmhousefare.co.uk

Producing a good

> **Did you know...**
>
> Job production is often associated with better quality products than those made using batch production methods. Farmhouse Fare, for example, stresses that its puddings are hand-made to encourage consumers to believe that the puddings are made one at a time. To emphasise their uniqueness, products made using job production are sometimes marketed as 'individually made'.

Hand finishing a cake

Methods of production

A large number of small manufacturing businesses make their products using job or batch production. The market for their products is usually not large enough to justify using mass production methods. Very large businesses such as Toyota, Dysons and Nokia use a different type of production. This method of production will be looked at in the next book.

Job production

Job production is when a single item is produced. The whole manufacturing process is completed before another item is made. The product might look the same as all the others, but it is probably unique. For example, when a new kitchen is fitted, the storage units will be standard size but the room itself will be different from other kitchens. The gas and water pipes will need to be adapted to fit and the kitchen storage units arranged to suit the room's shape.

Skilled workers will be required to complete the work. These workers will probably be well motivated as the work is not repetitive and boring. There will be problems for them to think about and solve throughout the whole fitting process. However, skilled labour is more expensive to employ. Also the nature of the work makes it **labour intensive**: this means there will be few opportunities to use equipment to do the work of labour.

Batch production

This is where a manufacturer makes a number, or batch, of products at the same time. Helen Colley uses **batch production** when cooking her puddings. The same equipment can be used to make the different types of puddings. This means there is less factory space required and there is no need to duplicate items of equipment. Farmhouse Fare might produce a batch of 2000 sticky toffee puddings then clean the equipment and make 1500 gingerbread and treacle puddings.

> **Did you know...**
>
> Some products combine the two methods of production. A baker might use batch production to make 40 cakes and then decorate each in a different way to appeal to different markets. Some might be boys' birthday cakes, some girls' birthday cakes, some anniversary cakes, and so on. These products might be described as 'hand-finished'.

Job production

Did you know…

When products are made in batches the batch number (or lot number) is often stamped on each item. This makes it easier to identify when the product was made. If there is a fault then all the other items in that batch can be checked.

Summary

- Small businesses usually use job or batch production
- Job production is suitable for making products that are unique
- Job production can be labour intensive
- Batch production involves making a number of identical items at once
- The work can be more repetitive for employees with batch production

Producing a good

Core knowledge

When a business is set up that will manufacture a product an important decision has to be made. Should the product be made one at a time, each being completed before the next is started? Or should several products be made together, in batches?

Sometimes there is no real choice. An artist who paints pictures for a living is unlikely to paint the same picture many times over. It would be unusual for an artist to paint the same sky on 30 pictures, followed by the same tree on each picture, and so on. The artist is more likely to paint one picture then start another. In this case job production would be used. A customer would not be impressed if she thought there were 29 similar pictures to the one that she had just bought.

A factory that produced pine furniture is more likely to use batch production methods. Rather than making just one chest of drawers at a time, the manufacturer will find it more economical to make, say, ten together. Ten lots of wood could be cut and used to make the frame. When these have been completed the wood for the drawers would be cut and assembled. When all ten chests of drawers had been made, they could all be varnished.

And more

Batch production can be a far more efficient way to make the puddings. Less skilful labour is needed, which is less expensive. There is also some opportunity to have employees specialise in a particular process. Someone could concentrate on the mixing of ingredients, while someone else looks after the baking process. The advantage of this is that workers become better at doing their own particular jobs.

Batch production may also require more equipment and machinery than job production. For example, a different tool might be needed for each stage of batch production to drill holes into metal. A worker making the product using job production would probably use the same drill, but just change the bit each time a different size hole was needed. More storage space is also required to keep the stock needed for making larger quantities of goods.

Another problem with batch production is that the work can become repetitive. A solution to this problem though would be to move employees between different jobs. This is known as job rotation.

Have a go!

Activity

Find a range of products that have a batch or lot number stamped on them. Produce a poster to explain what batch numbers are.

Group activity

Set up an experiment in your class. Create a design for a paper aeroplane (or something similar). Half the class should then produce as many planes as they can in, say 15 minutes. These should be made individually. In other words, each person works alone making a plane, finishing it before starting another. At the same time, the other half of the class splits up the manufacture of the plane into three or four different stages. The team then partly makes a number of the planes before the next stage is undertaken. The quality of each plane should be checked to see it is up to scratch. The numbers made by both types of processes can be compared.

Quickfire questions

1. What is meant by job production?
2. What is meant by batch production?
3. Why would a new pedestrian bridge across a road probably be made using job production?
4. Why do businesses put batch numbers on their products?
5. How can job rotation help make their work more interesting for employees?
6. Why would it be very expensive for Farmhouse Fare to make the puddings individually?
7. Why are batch numbers placed on products?
8. Why is batch production able to use less skilled workers than job production?
9. Describe how a florist making bouquets might use batch production.
10. Describe how Farmhouse Fare's puddings might be changed to suit the needs of different supermarkets.

Hit the spot

> Explain the differences between job and batch production.
> Give two advantages to a business of using batch rather than job production.
> Discuss the reasons why a business might choose not to use batch production.

Cracking the code

Batch production Making products a number at a time, rather than individually.

Diversify Operating in more than one market to reduce the risk to the business if one declines.

Factory A place where products are made.

Job production The process of completing one product before starting on another.

Labour intensive A process of making goods where many people are needed compared with the amount of machinery used.

Manufacturer A business that makes goods, rather than offers a service.

Chapter 27
Providing a service

IN THE NEWS

SportStars

James Taylor was given a £1000 cheque for his twenty-first birthday. The gift was meant to allow him to buy an around the world plane ticket. Instead, James used the money to start a business.

James' experiences as a sports coach in America after he had finished university persuaded him that there was a market for similar coaching in this country. James recognised that many children were not as active as they should be and childhood obesity was becoming a serious problem.

With his £1000 funding James bought some sporting equipment and started SportStars, his children's coaching venture. He managed to convince a small team of coaches to work for no pay until the business got established.

At the time SportStars was being planned, a law was introduced that allowed teachers 10 per cent of their working time away from the classroom to plan lessons and mark books. James realised that head teachers had to cover absent teachers and what better way than by providing sports coaching for the children? SportStars, therefore, targeted primary schools to find customers.

Appointments were set up with head teachers, where James explained the advantages of using SportStars. The coaches were cheaper to hire than supply teachers and the sporting activities fitted in well with the national project to improve children's health. SportStars also made sure that every child covered the requirements of the national curriculum.

A month of free trials led to five initial paid contracts. Word of mouth spread, the **contracts** grew in number and so did the SportStars product range. James introduced holiday courses where a venue was hired out for 11 weeks of the year and the kids came along for five hours every day.

At present James employs 15 full-time, 20 part-time, and up to 60 temporary coaches during the school holidays. Current **turnover** is around £1.2 million, and the company has offices in Cardiff, Bristol and Swansea, with plans to roll the service out across the UK, and even overseas.

@ Take a look at the Sportstars website at
www.sport-stars.co.uk

> **Did you know…**
>
> In 2008, financial and business services accounted for about one in five jobs in the UK, compared with about one in ten in 1981.

Service industries

James provides a service to schools. In return for a payment, he will provide a sports coach who will train the pupils. At the end of the lesson, the pupils should be better at sport and the school will feel that it has done something to make the children healthier. Neither the school nor the pupils will actually own something physical at the end of the day, as they would if they had bought a product from a business. This is what we mean by a service: something provided to a consumer at a point in time. The same would apply if you took a taxi ride, had a driving lesson, made a call on your mobile phone or had your hair cut at a hairdresser. These are all examples of services. Service industries sell directly to the customer or client and not to another business, which sells it on to the customer. Services are used up at the point they are delivered. They cannot be transferred to somebody else.

Many small businesses provide services

> **Did you know…**
>
> Some people believe that we now have a fourth type of industry: quaternary, which includes areas such as scientific research and intellectual property.

Summary

- James Taylor providing sports teachers to schools is an example of a service
- When a service is provided, nothing physical is given to the customer
- People pay for services because it often saves them having to do the work themselves

Providing a service

Core knowledge

Service industries are becoming increasingly important in the UK economy. Britain produces far fewer physical goods than it used to in the past. Let's take making cars as an example. Thirty years ago there were several UK car manufacturers producing hundreds of thousands of cars each year. Today, very few cars are made in the UK. Most of the cars on British roads have been built abroad and imported into this country. So Britain relies more on providing services as an industry. These services are sold both in Britain and abroad.

It was often thought that manufacturing industries were somehow better than service industries. This could be because something physical is made with manufacturing, which is not the case with services. Most people now recognise that a high proportion of wealth produced in services is a sign of an advanced economy.

A service industry

Even manufacturers, however, have to provide a service. More on this can be found in Chapter 29.

The main types of services

- *Financial* These include the services provided by banks and insurance companies. Banks will lend money and receive a rate of interest in return. Insurance companies will insure against unforeseen events, such as a car being damaged in an accident. People who want insurance pay a fee (called a premium) for this service. Many financial services are sold to people abroad.
- *Retailing* This is another way of saying 'shopping'. The retailer will sell products made by manufacturers to customers. It is a service as it saves consumers having to go to manufacturers to buy the goods that they want. The retailer does this for their customers and has the goods available in their shops.
- *Defence* We all want to feel protected and safe. The police and armed services, such as the army, provide us with the service of protection.
- *Education* Having an educated workforce is important if we are to grow as an economy. An education allows young people to become more capable of doing a wider range of jobs. Schools, colleges and universities provide the service of education. But there are many businesses that support education. SportStars is an example of such a business.
- *Health* Healthy people enjoy life better and live longer. There are many businesses that are involved in the health industry. Care homes for the elderly, medicine and drug manufacturers, doctors and dentists are just some of the ways the health service is provided.
- *Leisure* As people get better off they have more opportunity to enjoy their leisure time. Industries have grown up to provide leisure services to people. These include hotels, sporting facilities, eating out and travel.

> **And more**
>
> Sometimes services are called tertiary industries. Tertiary actually means third. Primary (or first) industries are those that obtain raw materials from the earth. Primary industries would, therefore, cover areas like mining, quarrying, forestry, farming and fishing. Secondary industries are the manufacturing industries – those that make products from the raw materials obtained from primary industries. Examples of secondary industries would be construction (building houses and factories), manufacturing washing machines and other domestic appliances, and furniture making.
>
> As economies develop, the proportion of primary, secondary and tertiary industries tend to change. Primary and secondary become less important and services, or tertiary, industries grow. Changes in technology can explain some of this change. Factories, for example, have machinery that replaces the number of workers needed. Information technology has made it easier to develop service industries. As just one example, computer technology has allowed banks to transfer money and manage people's accounts anywhere in the world. Britain can also buy raw materials and manufactured goods more cheaply abroad than they can be produced in the UK.
>
> Many people still worry that Britain relies so much on service industries. They believe that the move from secondary to tertiary (which is sometimes called **deindustrialisation**) means we depend too much on foreign countries producing goods for us. They also worry that if the economy is not doing very well, people cut back first on luxury items like staying in hotels and other leisure activities. This means that services are hit particularly badly when the economy is down turning.

Providing a service

Have a go!

Activity

Undertake a survey of the area in which you live. List the businesses in your area and mark each as a primary, secondary or tertiary industry. You may want to download a map of your area and mark on businesses with a colour code for each type.

Web-based activity

Go to the National Statistics website **www.statistics.gov.uk/glance**. Use this site to research the number of people who work in different types of industries.

Quickfire questions

1. Who started SportsStars?
2. Describe the service that SportStars provides to schools.
3. Give two examples of services that banks can provide to customers.
4. Which of these is not a service: a haircut; car insurance; replacement windows?
5. Explain why having security guards at a shopping centre is an example of a service.
6. Which service industry employed one person in five in 2008?
7. Explain two reasons why there are less people employed manufacturing goods.
8. Give two reasons why some people worry about the amount of service industries in the UK.
9. Explain how advances in ICT have helped financial services become more important.
10. Explain why it is important that Britain sells some of its services abroad.

Hit the spot

- Describe what is meant by a service.
- Describe the range of services provided by a leisure centre.
- Discuss whether all services are badly affected by the economy slowing down.

Cracking the code

Contract A legal agreement between a business supplying a service and the customer.
Deindustrialisation The movement away from manufacturing goods to providing services.
Turnover The money coming into a business from the goods and services it sells.

Chapter 28
Small businesses and ICT

IN THE NEWS

Streetcar

Andrew Valentine and Brett Akker got the idea for their different type of car rental business during a visit to America. After considering many options, the two university friends, came across the American Zipcars. The idea was simple: instead of having to go to the expense of buying and running a car, urban dwellers could hire a pay-as-you-go car just when they needed one. They could collect it from a range of parking sites, returning it when they had finished their journey. Calling their rental business Streetcar, the business's fleet of hire cars was originally based in London.

The attraction of pay-as-you-go car rental is that it is more convenient to customers. The cars are available 24 hours a day. The cars can be opened and the engine started with a **smart card** and number that is punched into the car's specially designed keypad. Membership of the scheme is £25 and there is an hourly rental fee to be paid. The cars are targeted at those who live in cities who only need a car occasionally for short periods. It is estimated that there are more than 1 million of these people in London alone.

In the beginning the entrepreneurs had just six cars in their fleet. This has now expanded to 125. The business is hoping to expand to other UK cities. The success of the scheme depends totally on the use of **ICT**.

After trawling the streets to find suitable premises to locate the cars, the founders have now established nearly 80 sites where users can access their vehicles. Valentine and Akker tracked down an overseas manufacturer who could cheaply produce the technology needed to allow secure use of the cars to genuine customers.

Streetcars used many aspects of ICT within the business. Including:

- Membership details are stored using smart card technology.
- Driving licence details are confirmed with the DVLA using telephone conference calling.
- Customers book a car online.
- Email and text messages are sent with details and confirmation.
- The car is opened with a smart card.
- Communication system in each car links to Streetcar base – allows mileage and costs to be debited from user's account.

Find out more about Streetcar at **www.streetcar.co.uk**.

Small businesses and ICT

> **Did you know...**
> The American Zipcars upon which Streetcar is based, was itself based on a car hire system that operated in Berlin in the 1990s.

> **Did you know...**
> Streetcar and similar car hire businesses might be the solution to traffic congestion in our major cities.

The advantages of ICT

The idea of hiring a car for short periods would be impossible without modern technology. Technology allows Streetcars to deal with its customers without ever meeting them personally. This would be unthinkable with a traditional car hire business, which would want to check the drivers' details before allowing them to rent a vehicle.

The use of ICT allows Streetcar to run with minimum operating costs. Once the technology has been bought, the business needs very few staff to keep it running. Technology that was unavailable just a few years ago now allows businesses to operate in quite different ways. Having a flexible system with minimum staffing means that customers can hire a car or van for as little as half an hour at a low hire charge.

Since starting the business, its owners have expanded beyond the London area. Streetcars can be found in Brighton, Southampton, Guildford, Kent and Cambridge. The scheme is particularly attractive in those towns and cities with heavy traffic congestion. It is estimated that for every Streetcar vehicle, six others are taken off the road, as they are no longer needed.

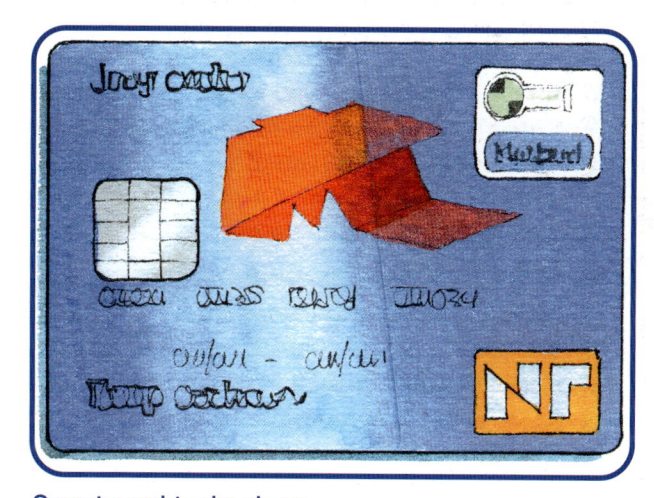

Smart card technology

> **Did you know...?**
> Cities with many students are prime locations for short-term car hire schemes.

Summary

- Without modern technology it would be impossible to operate a business like Streetcar
- Modern technology has allowed Streetcar to reduce the cost to the customer of hiring a car

Core knowledge

A computer is a standard feature of even the smallest business these days. Many do not go to the lengths that Streetcar goes to when using ICT but without ICT Streetcar would not be able to operate. Most businesses take advantage of the benefits that ICT offers and the main uses of ICT within a small business are explored below.

Record keeping

Businesses need to keep details of their customers and suppliers. Having these on a computer **database** means that they can be updated easily. Finding a phone number or contact name is much easier on a database than searching through a filing cabinet of records. Also it is easy to make a copy, so the records are less likely to get lost or destroyed.

Computers are essential in business today

Producing documents

Word processing has revolutionised the writing of business letters and memos. A business can store a series of standard letters on the computer to save having to type out similar documents over and over. The file with the required letter in can be opened and just the name and addressed changed. If many letters need to be sent, then a mail merge can be performed. This involves using details from a database to produce personalised letters.

Emails and the internet

Emails allow a business to send a message cheaply and quickly. Documents including photographs, maps, web pages and letters can be attached to messages. Small businesses can use the internet to advertise its products. The smallest business's website can be seen all over the world. The internet can also be used for market research purposes by keeping an eye on what the business's competitors are doing.

Other aspects of technology

Satellite navigation systems make it easier for deliveries to be made. This saves the business money and even shows the distance travelled so accurate delivery charges can be made. Online money transfers, such as PayPal, allow customers to pay for goods securely without waiting for the bank to clear the payment.

EPOS means Electronic Point of Sale. This is the system that allows readers to scan a barcode to record the product being sold and its price. The system allows the information from the barcode to be read quickly. EPOS systems can keep track of goods leaving the business so new stock can be ordered. While barcodes are found frequently in retailing, they can also be used to check the stock of a business and on parcels to show the address and postcode instantly.

Small businesses and ICT

> **And more**
>
> Most businesses want to be efficient. In simple terms this means getting the most from the available resources to the business. A business becomes more efficient when it produces more output from the same amount of inputs, or the same output from less inputs.
>
> Information technology has done much to increase the efficiency of businesses. Modern computer-controlled machines have reduced the level of skills employees need. This is sometimes called deskilling. In manufacturing, the work no longer needs someone who has served a long apprenticeship, as the machinery is mainly controlled by a computer. At one time a small business would have had a secretary to type letters. This service is no longer needed as word processing software allows documents of all sorts to be produced quickly and efficiently even by people who are not trained typists.
>
> ICT can be expensive in the short run. The business needs to pay for the hardware (computers, printers, etc.) and for training staff. In the long run, however, this investment will probably pay for itself in terms of lower costs.

Have a go!

Web-based activities

Go to the Streetcar website and another car hire company. Compare the prices charged by each company.

Produce a web page showing the benefits of Streetcar to the occasional car user, living in London.

Quickfire questions

1. What makes Streetcar different from other car hire businesses?
2. How does Streetcar know how many miles each customer has driven?
3. How does Streetcar use smart card technology?
4. Give a reason why so many of Streetcar's vehicles are mainly based in London.
5. Why would a traditional car hire company find it difficult to hire vehicles for just 30 minutes?
6. What is a standard letter?
7. Give two uses of the internet to small businesses.
8. Describe how a used car dealer might use a database of his customers.
9. Explain how EPOS can help a supermarket avoid running out of a product.
10. A customer leaves her name and address when she buys a new computer. Explain two ways the retailer might use this information.

Hit the spot

- Describe two ways a small business might use ICT to reduce its costs.
- Explain two ways in which ICT has changed the way that people work.
- Discuss whether it is appropriate for businesses to send spam emails and SMS messages to customers.

Cracking the code

Database A store of electronic information, such as customers' names and addresses.

ICT Information and communication technology.

Smart cards Pocket-size cards with a computer chip that contains information.

Chapter 29
The importance of customer service

IN THE NEWS

Tours4.com

Tours4 is a sports tour and group travel operator that was set up in 2005. The small business started by organising travel, accommodation and sporting fixtures for UK teams that wanted to play abroad.

Twenty-four-year-old Daniel Smith and his business partner Sam Jennings met when they were working as language teachers in French schools. Both were keen sportsmen and had organised football and rugby tours from the UK to play with French teams. The feedback they received from the players was very good, so the pair considered turning to tour organising as a career.

The Manchester and Kent-based business has diversified and in addition now organises stag and hen celebrations, often to major European locations. Many of the sporting tours last for 4–7 days, but an increasing number of events are for shorter periods of time. Tours4 offers shorter, often single day, visits to theatres, comedy clubs, ice rinks and paintballing venues. Tours4 is also moving into the school market, with events such as skiing holidays.

Daniel and Sam did a lot of **market research** before starting Tours4. They were particularly concerned to get the pricing right, and to check the level of service that they offered to customers was

Satisfied customers

appropriate. To achieve this, they contacted players and managers of sports teams at schools, clubs and universities throughout the UK to ask for their opinions.

Young people pay between £50 and £1000 for a sports tour, depending on where it is and the duration of the tour. In return they expect a smooth event, coaches on time, accommodation booked and an opportunity to relax and enjoy themselves. Accommodation does not have to be 5-star standard. Young people tend not to want the tour to be over-organised, with guides telling them what to do.

Take a look at **www.tours4.com**.

> **Did you know...**
>
> It is said that it costs between five and six times more to attract a new customer than to keep an existing one and companies can boost profits anywhere from 25 to 125 per cent by retaining merely 5 per cent more existing customers.

Customer satisfaction

Tours4 is often used to save sports teams having to organise their own trips. Sports teams are prepared to rely on Tours4's expertise in organising this type of event. It is even possible that the tours will be cheaper, as Tours4 will probably get **discounts** the clubs would not receive when organising the tour themselves.

What most of Tours4 customers want is a guide, someone who can speak the language. They also want the reassurance of someone on a phone in the UK in case there is a problem.

A school sports tour will be looking for different levels of service than group of young people on a stag or hen night, or university students going paintballing. The school taking the tour will need to reassure parents that the trip is safe and well organised. It is for this reason that Daniel and Sam are prepared to visit schools to talk about the arrangements with parents.

Most of Tours4 clients are young people, quite often students. Tours4 need to make sure that the services that they offer these people suits their needs. What the young people are looking for is a good time, with plenty of fun activities. They will not be too worried about the state of the accommodation; there will be no need for 5-star hotels and the students will be happy to share rooms to keep costs down.

If Tours4 is successful in providing good customer service, then the level of customer satisfaction will be high. Customer satisfaction means people feel that they have had a good experience on the tour. The service was at a standard customers were expecting, or even better than this. Customers also feel that they have had good value for money.

Customer satisfaction is important to a business like Tours4. The business relies on word of mouth advertising. If a group had a good tour with them, they would tell others. This would encourage other teams to use the service. A poor trip would, of course, have the opposite effect. Tours4 also wants to get its customers to use its services again. Having a good experience will stop teams going to other operators when they book their next tour.

Different customers have different needs

> **Did you know...**
>
> It is said that happy customers tell four to five others of their positive experience. Dissatisfied customers tell nine to twelve how bad it was.

The importance of customer service

Did you know...
It is said that two-thirds of customers do not feel valued by those serving them.

Summary

- A successful business needs to offer a good service to its customers
- If customers are satisfied with the service they receive, they are more likely to return and to tell their friends
- **Customer satisfaction** comes from making the customers feel special, giving them what they want and offering value for money

Core knowledge

A good business would want to know how satisfied its customers are with the service that was provided. Often, businesses will ask customers for feedback, so they can find out how successful they have been. Market research can also provide businesses with ideas of how the service can be improved; so future customers are more likely to be satisfied.

There are several ways in which businesses can help improve the level of customer satisfaction:

Customer service This means giving personal attention to make the customers feel important. Customers are most likely to appreciate the goods and services that they buy if they are made to feel special. This occurs when they feel that the goods and services that they buy have been specially produced for them.

Quality of service This does not necessarily mean the best quality. Tours4's customers would not expect expensive hotels, for example. But the service should be at least as good as the customer expects.

After sales service Nobody wants to feel that they have been forgotten about when the bill has been paid. Businesses can following up with after sales support. This may be something as simple as a questionnaire or a phone call, asking if everything went well. Manufacturers could provide maintenance and updating. A computer software business, for example, might want to provide updates to packages when they are available.

Excellent customer service

And more

Some businesses go as far as to measure the level of customer satisfaction. This can be achieved with survey techniques and questionnaires. A major problem with customer surveys, however, is that the response rate can be very low. This can produce distorted results, as people who have had a poor experience are far more likely to respond to the survey. The questionnaires also must be straightforward and not too lengthy. A long, complicated form would put people off completing it.

AQA BUSINESS FOR GCSE: SETTING UP A BUSINESS

Have a go!

Activity

Create a questionnaire that could be used to measure customer satisfaction. The business could be one used by students at your school or college. This could be a local leisure centre, cinema or a shop. Ask people to complete the questionnaire and present your findings to the class.

Web-based activity

Go on to the Tours4 website. Produce a flyer that could be sent to schools advertising the business. Stress the level of service that the business offers when arranging trips for schools.

Quickfire questions

1. What type of business is Tours4?
2. Who are Tours4's main customers?
3. Describe two ways Tours4 offers a good service to its customers.
4. Give two reasons why schools might choose to use Tours4, rather than organising a skiing trip themselves.
5. Describe a way in which market research can help a business improve its service.
6. Give an advantage and a disadvantage of a business relying on word of mouth advertising.
7. Explain what after-sales service a painter and decorator might offer his customers.
8. What benefits could an improvement in service bring to a business?
9. Use the Tours4 case study to help explain what is meant by an appropriate standard of quality.
10. Discuss how a school offers a service to the parents of students.

Hit the spot

> What is meant by customer satisfaction?
>> Explain two ways in which a business could improve the level of its customers' satisfaction.
>>> Discuss whether a business can accurately measure the amount of satisfaction its customers get.

Cracking the code

Customer satisfaction A measure of how pleased a customer is with a service or good.
Discount Reduction in price often given to regular or large spending customers.
Market research Investigating potential customers or competitors. Looking at issues such as what customers want and the price they are prepared to pay.

Chapter 30
Protecting the consumer

IN THE NEWS

Trading Standards

Unfortunately not all businesses operate in a fair and honest manner. Throughout history there have been many examples of businesses that have tried to cheat customers in one way or another. This could be something as simple as selling underweight items. An unscrupulous trader might have adjusted his scales so they weigh his products heavier than should be the case. There are other ways in which customers can be cheated. The trader might describe the product unfairly, saying things about it that simply aren't true.

To overcome these sorts of problems, various governments over the years have set up organisations to monitor business and protect the **consumer**. One of these government organisations is **Trading Standards**. One issue that Trading Standards is particularly concerned about these days is the growth in counterfeit goods.

Counterfeit goods are illegally copied items that are passed off for sale as the genuine article. These copied goods are normally an inferior product, but rely on the selling power of the brand. The main items that are counterfeited are:

- designer labelled clothing, sportswear, perfume, watches and equipment;
- CD and DVD copies of popular films and chart-topping music;
- computer software, especially games and business programs;
- artistic works, such as paintings, pottery and models.

Counterfeit goods may be sold at car boot sales or markets

Trading Standards departments take very seriously the production, distribution and sale of counterfeit products. The organisation has many of the powers of police in entering premises, seizing illegal goods and arresting those involved with counterfeiting.

There are many reasons for taking such a tough approach. Many brands are Trade Marks ™ or protected by copyright ©. Using these brands without permission is illegal. Unsuspecting customers might buy the copies in good faith. But when things go wrong with the product they find there is no after-sales support or guarantees provided. As the products are usually made from inferior materials, the items could even be dangerous to use.

@ Take a look at the Trading Standards website:
www.tradingstandards.gov.uk

> **Did you know…**
> A good way to spot counterfeit items of clothing is to check the labels and packaging. Many of these contain basic spelling mistakes.

Consumer legislation

The laws on counterfeited goods are just one of the ways in which consumers are protected. Over the years there has been other legislation.

Sale of Goods Act

One of the most powerful laws is the Sale of Goods Act. This states that goods sold must be:

- 'Fit for purpose' – which means the product should do what it is meant to do. A jacket that is described as machine washable must be able to go through the washing machine without being damaged.

- 'Satisfactory quality' – this means that there should not be any faults with the product. A pair of jeans with stitching that was coming away would not be of satisfactory quality. However, if the fault were pointed out before the sale took place, then the customer must accept that the product is seconds quality.

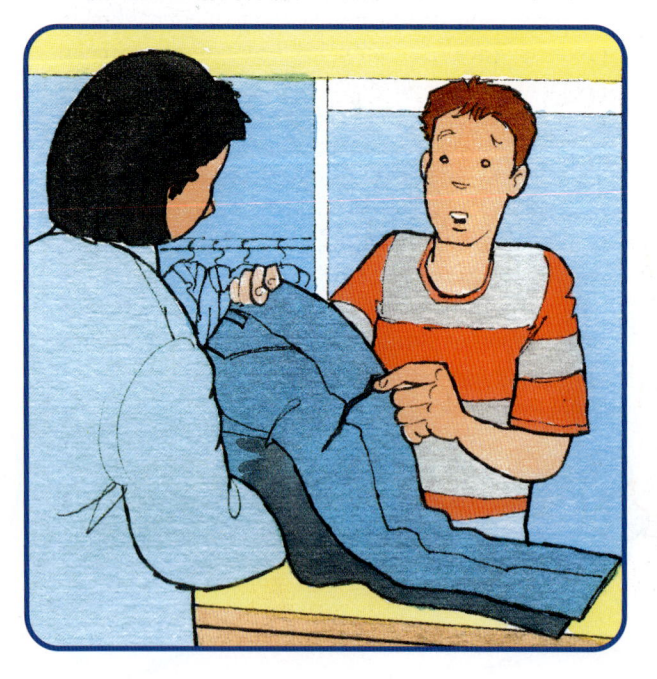

Trade Descriptions Act

Another law protecting consumers is the Trade Descriptions Act. This controls how goods can be promoted in advertising or on packaging. To describe a car as having had only one previous owner, when there had been three, would be breaking the law.

Food and toy safety

These are special laws that apply to particular products. The government feels that both toy and food production deserve special attention. Environmental Health officers have the power to check conditions in places that prepare food and to close these places down if they do not meet certain standards. Similarly, quality and safety are important when manufacturing toys. There are rules about materials that are used in toys. Toys have to pass certain tests to prove that they are safe when young children play with them.

Quality and safety are very important

Protecting the consumer

Did you know…

It is estimated that in Britain more than £10 billion is lost through the illegal sale of counterfeit goods.

Summary

- There are a range of laws that protect consumers from being cheated by businesses
- There are laws that ensure that goods and services sold meet certain basic standards
- Sellers must describe their goods and services accurately

Core knowledge

Customers do not want to feel that they have been cheated in some way by a business. Most of us take reasonable care to look after our own interests. We won't return to a business whose service or product we are not happy with. Many of us will complain if we do not get the service that we expect from a business.

When you pay for a service you are entitled to certain standards. For instance, imagine you are having your car serviced. The job should be done to a proper standard of workmanship. You should expect the car not to break down the day after the service. If your car developed a fault not long after you had bought it with a guarantee or warranty, it is not unreasonable to expect it to be repaired promptly. If you have to have a repair to the car and had not agreed a price beforehand, the price charged should be reasonable.

AQA BUSINESS FOR GCSE: SETTING UP A BUSINESS

> **And more**
>
> You might find it strange that some people believe that not only is consumer protection unnecessary, but it is actually bad for consumers. Some of their arguments are:
>
> - Producers of branded goods charge high prices, so they are beyond the reach of many consumers. Counterfeiting these branded goods makes them less attractive to consumers who were willing to pay high prices. So in order to sell their goods the brand producers have to lower their prices, allowing more people to be able to afford them.
> - Operating consumer protection laws costs a great deal of money. Trading Standard officers need to be paid, just as one example. To fund this spending the government will increase taxes that people have to pay.
> - A need for consumer protection suggests that consumers are unable to look after their own interests. If consumers are cheated, they will not go back to the business that cheated them. The business would get a bad reputation, losing custom and eventually closing. The rule of letting customers look after their own interests is very old. It is given the Latin name, *caveat emptor*, which means 'Let the buyer beware'.
>
> But there are other issues as well. It is not unusual for unscrupulous traders to copy safety marks on to clothing to make them more attractive to consumers. Children's clothing might be marked as flame resistant when it is not.
>
> As goods become more technologically advanced, it's not always easy to spot faults in a product. If you are buying a new bike that is meant to have an aluminium frame, carbon forks and aerodynamic spokes in the wheels, can you be sure you are getting just that, or inferior materials?

Protecting the consumer

Have a go!

Activities

Produce a quiz based on *Who Wants to be a Millionaire?* The questions should all be about consumer protection.

Research the British Standards Institute (BSI). Produce a PowerPoint presentation on the work of this organisation.

Web-based activity

Go on to the Trading Standards website **www.tradingstandards.gov.uk** and produce a leaflet on consumers' rights when buying goods.

Quickfire questions

1. What are counterfeited goods?
2. What is the function of the Trading Standards?
3. A shop sells a radio alarm clock. Use this to explain the meaning of fit for purpose.
4. Draw three examples of trademarks that you have seen.
5. Explain how a vacuum cleaner might be seen as not being of satisfactory quality.
6. Give two reasons why trading standards officers might close down a restaurant.
7. Give two ways in which a manufacture of mobile phones might break the Trade Descriptions Act.
8. Explain why the producers of branded goods are keen to stop counterfeit copies being made.
9. Explain two possible reasons why toys are a particular concern for trading standards.
10. Explain why some people do not believe that consumer protection laws are needed.

Hit the spot

▸ What is meant by consumer protection?
▸ Explain how stopping counterfeit goods being sold can help the consumer.
▸ Discuss the arguments both for and against having consumer protections laws.

Cracking the code

Consumer Someone who buys goods and services.

Trading Standards A government organisation that looks after consumers to stop them from being cheated.

Preparing for the controlled assessment

What is a controlled assessment?

Controlled assessments have replaced coursework across all awarding bodies, including AQA. Unlike coursework, there are some restrictions (or controls) which your teacher has to ensure are in place while you do the work.

Your hard work on this GCSE course will be assessed by a combination of exams and controlled assessments.

Why is the controlled assessment needed?

The one-hour exam paper that you sit for each unit of study cannot assess all of the assessment objectives thoroughly.

The controlled assessment gives you the time to show the examiner just how good you are at using business ideas, when you have more time to think carefully about the issues. In the past this was done using coursework, but schools found that coursework took too long to produce, taking away valuable learning time. The controlled assessment was designed to take less time.

Which assessments do I need to do?

The assessments you do will depend on the course you are taking.

- A **short GCSE** business studies course (your school may call this a **half**-**GCSE**): you have to take a controlled assessment and one exam.
- The **full GCSE** course: two exam papers and a controlled assessment. This assessment is slightly different from the short course version. More details on your controlled assessment can be found in the Unit 2 textbook.
- The **double award GCSE** in Applied Business: you do not need to take a controlled assessment for this part of the award, so count your blessings, but remember you will have other assessments to do later.

The controlled assessment is a significant part of your GCSE. Your final GCSE grade will be greatly influenced by how well you do in this assessment:

- The Unit 14 controlled assessment makes up 40% of the final grade for the short course GCSE.
- The Unit 3 controlled assessment makes up 25% of the final grade for the full course GCSE.

The Unit 14 controlled assessment

The controlled assessment for the **short course GCSE** is called Unit 14: Investigating small businesses. (Remember that, if you are taking the full course or the double award, you will take a different assessment, not this one.)

'Investigating small businesses' is a very general title. Before you start your course, the awarding body, AQA, will set a more specific task that you will need to complete under controlled conditions – the controlled assessment. It will include a case study or scenario relating to the topics you learn about during the course.

The task changes each year. This means if you need to re-sit the controlled assessment, you will be tackling a different task the second time.

AQA publish details of the latest controlled assessment each year: they send the details to teachers and publish them on the web notice board for Business Studies.

Preparing for the controlled assessment

Table of assessments for the different courses: who does what

Note: Each exam mentioned here lasts one hour.

	Exam: Setting up a business (Unit 13)*	Exam: Setting up a business (Unit 1)	Controlled assessment: Investigating small businesses (Unit 14)	Exam: Growing as a business (Unit 2)	Controlled assessment: Investigating businesses (Unit 3)	Other assessments
Short course GCSE	✓		✓			
Full course GCSE		✓		✓	✓	
Double-award GCSE		✓				✓

* Unit 13 covers the same material as Unit 1, and everything you need to know is covered in this book. However, the Unit 13 exam paper will have different questions to the Unit 1 paper.

Your teacher will give you information about the controlled assessment task when he or she feels the time is right.

If you would like to research more about this assessment, then you will find plenty of information on the AQA website, www.aqa.org.uk. The fastest way to find the information is to do a search on the site for 'GCSE business studies controlled assessment 2012' (if you are taking your exams and controlled assessment in 2012).

Carrying out the assessment

There are two stages to the controlled assessment:
- Planning and researching the topics covered in the assignment.
- Writing up the assignment.

Planning and research

You teacher should only set you off on the assignment once you have been taught the material that it covers. For example, if the assignment scenario deals with marketing, then you need to be familiar with the marketing section of this book before you start to work. Your assignment research should relate to the particular details of the assignment, not the basic terms.

During the planning stage, you will be allowed to work with other students, if your teacher thinks that this is suitable for you and your class. (The next stage, writing up, is done under test conditions.)

You are advised by AQA to spend between five and eight hours preparing for the task. During this time you are expected to be able to:

- Select relevant information from a variety of sources.
- Explain what you have discovered in your research, and **why** you chose to do the research in the way that you did. For instance, if the scenario is about an entrepreneur thinking about starting a small service sector business, you may be required to conduct some market research into the service to be provided.
- Consider the methods that would be suitable for that type of business, and possibly actually conduct the market research yourself.

- Support your choice of method when you write up the assessment, as well as outlining your actual findings.
- Explore any issues that have been raised in your research. For example, if a business has a choice between two options, such as lowering its prices to attract customers, or advertising more instead, you will have to put forward clear points for and against both options in order to score well.

Keep careful notes of all your findings during this stage of the assessment, as these notes can be used when you write up.

You are allowed to ask for help from your teacher at this stage in the assessment. They may, for instance, get you to look at alternative ways of thinking about the topic or solving the problem. They may also provide guidance on sources of information, maybe by suggesting a website to visit. Your teacher, however, has to let AQA know exactly what type of assistance has been given to you.

Writing up the assignment

You will have up to three hours to write up your assignment. This time is not fixed; it is just a recommendation from AQA. You are allowed more time, but it shouldn't be necessary. Extra time is available if you have special educational needs, and this will be explained to you by your school.

AQA is not looking for very long and rambling answers. It is possible to score high marks with brief pieces of work that get straight to the point and show your skills of application, analysis and evaluation.

Your teacher will probably run the writing-up time in more than one session, probably during normal timetabled lessons. If there is more than one session, you will not be allowed to take any of your notes or your written work out of the room between sessions. This material must be collected by your teacher and kept safe until the next session.

During the writing time, you will need to complete the task that has been set by AQA. This may take the form of a presentation or a report, or some other style of presenting your findings. You may be able to produce your account on a computer, but hand-written responses are just as good.

You will need to sign a declaration when you hand in your assignment to say that your assessment is your own work

How is the assessment marked?

Your teacher will give your work a mark out of 60. Teachers will be looking for three skills, called Assessment Objectives (see table).

The teacher will also assess your ability to write good quality English and present clear arguments. This is known as the quality of written communication (QWC). Writing with few spelling or other mistakes will be rewarded. You will also score well on QWC if you are able to use business terms as you write.

Once your work has been marked by your teacher, AQA will ask for a sample of the work or, in some cases, all the students' work to be sent away. This is simply to check that everyone's work has been marked to the same standard, whichever school they are at.

Assessment objective (AO)	Maximum marks
AO1: having knowledge and understanding of business ideas and terms	21 marks
AO2: being able to apply, or use, these business ideas and terms to explain the issues in your assignment	25 marks
AO3: showing evidence that you have brought in business ideas to explore the information that you have collected. You also need to make judgements on how useful this evidence is.	14 marks

Index

Note: page numbers in **bold** refer to key word definitions.

above-the-line expenditure 80
accountants
   financial 108, 120
   management 108, 120
accounting, and predictions 111–12
accounts 53, 104–9
   appropriation 112
   profit and loss 111–12
adding value 75
Adult Learning Grants 101
advertising 79–80, 82–3, **84**
   revenue 104
advice 15–16, 99
after sales service 167
age discrimination 140
Age Discrimination Act 2006 140
AIDA 82–3, **84**
AIM (Alternative Investment Market) 26
air travel 68–9
Akker, Brett 160
Andrew, Prince, Duke of York 2
application forms 124, 127, **128**
Articles of Association 53
assets 46, 106, 118
   definition **49**, **109**, **122**
   written down 93
augmented product 75
awareness-raising 82

B2B (business-to-business) transactions 12
balance sheets 108
Balon, Adam 50
bankruptcy 46–7, **49**
banks
   advice from 99
   loans 41, 43, 93, 95
barcodes 162
bartering 3
batch numbers 152

batch production 150, 151–2, 153, **154**
BBC (British Broadcasting Corporation) 80
BBC iPlayer 73–4
BCC (British Chambers of Commerce) 101
below-the-line expenditure 80
Bigger Feet 40, 41
billionaires 15
Body Shop 16, 21
BOGOF (Buy One Get One Free) 82
bonuses 130, **133**
boredom 137, 152
BP 2
brands 11, 21, 22, 76
Branson, Richard 16, 47, 51, 130
bread 8
break even 29, 111, 113, **115**
   graphs 113
'bricks and clicks' 89
Bridge, Oliver 40, 41
British Broadcasting Corporation *see* BBC
British Chambers of Commerce (BCC) 101
Brown, Chinelo 98
BSM (British School of Motoring) 21
budgets 107–8
business
   definition 2–7, **7**
   reasons for 3–4, **5**
Business Active (magazine) 104
business advice 15–16, 99
business aims 5, 26–32, **32**, 112
business angels 51, **54**, 94
business cards 81
business failure 23, 41, 43, 46–7, 52, 95, 118
business growth/expansion 21, 22, 29

Business Link 99, 101
business location 55–60
business models 23
business objectives 26–32, **32**
business planning 40–4, **44**, 120
business plans 40–4, **44**
business size 2, 80
Business Start Up Scheme 99
business structure 45–9
   limited liability 48, 50–4, 131
   unlimited liability 46–8
business support 98–103
   formal 98–101
   informal 99
business targets 27–9, 111
business-to-business (B2B) transactions 12
buying, core/secondary reasons for 75
Byshiem, Cat 98

capital 51, **54**, 106
   venture 17, 94
capital depreciation 105
car manufacturing 15, 157
car rental businesses 160–1
carbon footprints 30
Carluccio, Antonio 26–7
cash deficits 118, 120, **122**
cash flow 116–22, **148**
   forecasts 42, 118, 120
   inflows 120
   net 117
   outflows 120
   statements 108, 120
   tables 117, 118
cash surplus 120, **122**
catering 26–7, 71, 150
   see also fast-food
caveat emptor (buyer beware) 172
chain of distribution 88, **90**

Index

Chambers of Commerce 101
change, product 74–5, 77
charitable donations 134
charts 63, 113
chefs 26
China 8, 9
chip and pin cards 12
cinema 74
Citizens Advice Bureau 99
Clark, Nyree 98
Coca-Cola 27
Coffee Nation 34, 36, 58
Colley, Helen 150, 151
communication 134, 136
communities 36, 37–8, **39**
Companies House 53
competition 10, 70–1, 74–5
   and business location 57, 58
   non-price 10, **13**
   price 10, **13**
   and the product life cycle 76
   and profit 113
   researching your 63–4
competitions 66
construction industry 71, 92, 144
consumer goods 76, **78**
   consumables 6, 76
   consumer durables 6, 76
consumer legislation 171
consumer protection 169–72
consumers 169, **173**
contingencies 93, **97**
contracted hours 130, **133**
contracts 155, **159**
copyright 99, **103**, 169
corporate social responsibility (CSR)
   28, 30, **32**, 134
cosmetic changes 75, 77, **78**
cost plus pricing 70
costs 104, 107, 125
   and break-even 111
   and cash flow 116, 118, 120
   definition **109**
   distribution 87, 104
   fixed 93, 107, 113
   overheads 112, **115**
   and place 87
   and profit 111, 112, 113
   running 107, **109**, 112
   start-up (sunk) 107, **109**

total 113
   variable 93, 107, 113
counterfeit goods 169–71
Country Estates Garden (CEG)
   Furniture 129, 130, 132
courts, small claims 144, 145–7
cover price 104
credit 36, 46, **49**, 96
   formal 93
   informal 93
credit cards 95
creditors 46, 52, 118
   and bad debt 145–7
   definition **39**, **49**, **54**, **122**, **148**
   as stakeholders 36, **39**
customer analysis 66, **67**
customer feedback 64, 65, 167
customer profiling 66, 81
customer satisfaction 29, 166–7, **168**
customer service 165–8
customers 35–6, 37

data 64
   qualitative 66
   quantitative 66
databases 162, **164**
debt 46–7, 92, 93, 94
   bad 144, 145–7
   charging interest on 147
   limited liability for 51, 52
   recovery in the small claims court
      144, 145–7
   writing off 147, **148**
debtors 146, **148**
Deering Brothers builders 92
deficits 118, 120, **122**
defining business and enterprise
   1–32
   aims and objectives 5, 26–32, **32**
   business 2–7, **7**
   enterprise 14–19, **19**
   franchises 20–5, **25**
   markets 8–13
deindustrialisation 158, **159**
demand 5, 9, 11, **13**, 63, 71
desire 11, 83
deskilling 163
Digital Rights Management (DRM)
   software 73
directors 52

disability discrimination 139, 140
Disability Discrimination Act 2004 140
discounts 129, 130, **133**, 166, **168**
discrimination 139, 140, 142
distribution 86–8, **90**
   chain of 88, **90**
   costs 87, 104
   long channel 88
diversification 150, **154**
dividends 35, **39**, 131
document production 162
dot com businesses 89
downloads 85
Dragon's Den (TV show) 17, 18, 79
DRM (Digital Rights Management)
   software 73
DVDs 74, 75

e-commerce 40, 87–8, 89
e-crime 12
easyJet 68
economies of scale 21
education 157
Education Sense 124, 125
efficiency 163
EFTPOS (Electronic Funds Transfer at
   Point of Sale) 12, **13**
Electronic Point of Sale (EPOS) 162
email 162
employees 48
   and business location 56–7
   full-time 125
   and the law 139–43
   motivating 134–8
   part-time 125, 141
   recruitment 124–8
   rewarding 129–33
   skilled 56–7
   as stakeholders 35, 37
employer's liability insurance 145
employment laws 139, 140–2, **143**
endorsement 83
enterprise 14–19, **19**
   culture of 100
   planning 40–4
Enterprise Areas 102
Enterprise Strategy 100
enthusiasm 16
entrepreneurs 14–17, **19**, 100
   and business planning 41, 43

Index 179

and financing 41
and limited liability 51
locating businesses 56, 57, 58
qualities of 15–16
and unlimited liability 46–8
young 14, 15, 40
Environmental Health Officers 170
environmental issues 30, 37–8
EPOS (Electronic Point of Sale) 162
ethical business 30, **32**
ethical investment 30
European Union (EU) 99
expenditure 108
   above-the-line 80
   below-the-line 80
expenses 112, **115**

factories 150, **154**
factors of production 106
fairtrade 30, 34
Farmhouse Fare 150, 151
fast-food 20, 23, 62
fees, franchising 21, **25**
Ferguson, Sarah, Duchess of York 2
file-sharing (peer-to-peer) sites 85
finances 41, 42, 50–1, 91–122
   accounts 104–9
   business support 98–103
   cash flow 116–22
   profit 110–15
   sources of 92–7, 100, 102, **103**
financial accountants 108, 120
financial services 157
fireworks 119
'fit for purpose' 170
flexible working hours 142
flyers 81–2
focus groups 65
food
   and consumer protection 170
   distribution 9
   prices 8
   see also catering; fast-food
food miles 30
Ford, Henry 15
Foster, Claire 98
franchisees 21, 23, **25**
franchisers 21, 23, **25**
franchises 20–5, **25**
   advantages 21

disadvantages 22
fees 21, **25**
royalties 21, 22, **25**
standards 24
turnover 21, **25**
fraud 12
fringe benefits 130, 131, 136
full-time employees 125

Gannon, Karl 124
gaps in the market 10–11, 62, 63, **67**
Gnarls Barkley 85
goods 4–6, 76
   and consumer protection 170–1
   improved 17
   new 16–17
   production 150–4
grants 99, 101, 102
Grants and Support Directory 102
graphs 63
Griffiths, Oliver 98
Grocer, The (magazine) 8
guarantees 66
guarantors 40, **44**

hard workers 16
Harrison, Joel 110, 111
head hunting 127
Health and Safety at Work Act (1974) 142
Health and Safety Executive (HSE) 142
health services 157
Heinz 27
hire purchase 96, **97**
Hitchings, Carl 55
HM Revenue and Customs 99, 145, **148**
home delivery 87
housing 92
'hub and spoke' systems 68
hygiene factors 137, **138**

ICT (information and communication technology) 160–4, **164**
ideas, new 15, 16, 41
identity theft 12
income 107, 111
   highest earning occupations 130
   see also salaries; wages

incorporation 51, 52, 53
industrial inertia 58, **60**
Industrial Tribunals 142, **143**
information 64
   electronic 65
infrastructure 56, 58
Innocent Smoothies 50
innovation 28, 100
inputs 5–6
insurance 145
interest 147
interest-free borrowing 95
Internet 9, 12, 162
   BBC iPlayer 73–4
   and market research 63–4
   music downloads 85
   online money transfer systems 162
   and promotion 83
   shopping 56
   usage trends 71
interviews 65, 127, **128**
investment 17
   ethical 30
   and limited liability 52–3
invoices 144, **148**

Jennings, Sam 165
job advertisements 126
job application forms 124, 127, **128**
Job Centres 45, **49**
job interest 137
job interviews 127, **128**
job production 151, 153, **154**
job rotation 152
job satisfaction 132
job security 125
Jobcentres 126

Kellogg's 8, 9, 10–11

labour 4, 106
   skilled 151
   turnover 28, **32**
labour intensive work 151, **154**
land 106
law
   consumer protection 171–2
   staff and the 139–43
   see also legal responsibilities of business

Index

leaflets 81–2
Learning and Skills Council (LSC) 101
leasing equipment 48
legal responsibilities of business 144–8
   see also law
leisure services 157
liability
   limited 48, 50–4, 108, 131
   unlimited 46–8
limited liability companies 48, 50–4, 131
   accounts 108
   private limited companies 51, 52
   public limited companies 51, 52, 108
liquidity 147, **148**
Little Theatre, Dale 116, 118, 119
loans 41, 43, 93–5, 100
   long-term 94
   medium-term 94
   short-term 93
Local Authorities 101
local communities 36, 37–8, **39**
local councils 57
local newspapers 81
loss 113
loss leaders 70
loyalty 134, **138**
LSC (Learning and Skills Council) 101

management
   and business plans 41–2
   maximising expertise 28
management accountants 108, 120
manpower 28
manufacturing 4, 150, **154**, 157–8
mark-ups 70
market maps 11, **13**
market research 40, 43, **44**, 47, 62–7, 165, **168**
   continuing 64
   methods 63
   and new technology 63–4
   primary 64, 65, **67**
   purpose 63
   secondary 65, **67**
market segments 17

market share 29
market trends 74, 75
marketing 28, 61–90
marketing budget 69
marketing mix
   balance 71
   definition 69, **72**
   place 69, 85–91, **90**
   price 68–72
   product 69, 73–8
   promotion 69, 70, 71, 76, 79–84
markets 8–13, 17
   and business location 56
   and business plans 42
   competitive 10
   gaps in the 10–11, 62, 63, **67**
   mass 10, 87
   niche 10, 87
   and price 8, 9–11
   and promotion 81
   target 87, **90**
   virtual 9, 12
Marsden, Stephen 62
mass markets 10, 87
mass production 15
'matched funding' 102, **103**
maternity leave 141
maximising 28, 112, **115**
McDonald's 22
Memorandum of Association 53
mentors 99, **103**
middle men 110
millionaires 15
minimising 28
minimum wage 131, 139, **143**
mission statements 26, 27, **32**
mobile businesses 105
money 3, 15, 41
money transfer systems, online 162
mortgages 94, **97**
motivation 134–8
multinationals 2
music industry 85

National Express 24
National House Building Council 92
national minimum wage 131, 139, **143**
needs 3, 5, 11
New Entrepreneur Scholarship 45, **49**

newspapers, local 81
niche markets 10, 87
non-price competition 10, **13**

observation 65
occupations, highest earning 130
Office for National Statistics (ONS) 23, 66
online money transfer systems 162
operations management 149–73
   consumer protection 169–73
   customer service 165–8
   goods production 150–4
   service provision 155–9
   small businesses and ICT 160–4
output 5–6, 111
overdrafts 93, **97**
overdrawn 144, **148**
overheads 112, **115**
overtime 129, 130, **133**
'owner's own funds' 93, 95, **97**

Palmair 69
parents 142
part-time employees 125, 141
passing trade 55, **60**
patents 99, **103**
paternity leave 141
pay-as-you-go car rental 160–1
PayPal 162
pensions 131
people in business 123–48
   legal responsibilities of business 144–8
   motivating employees 134–8
   rewarding staff 129–33
   staff and the law 139–43
   staff recruitment 124–8
performance-related pay 132
perks 134, **138**
persistence 16
personal recommendations 80, 81, 127
piecework 132, **133**
planning 40–4, **44**, 120
policies 34, **39**
positive discrimination 142, **143**
Post-it notes 17
posters 81–2

Index

predictions, 'what if' 111–12
premises 56, **60**, 88
price 8, 9–11, 68–72
  changes 9
  competition 10, **13**
  cost plus pricing 70
  cover price 104
  of food 8
  lowering 71
  mark-ups 70
  promotional 70, 80
  psychological point pricing 69
primary industries 158
Prince's Trust, The 45, **49**, 98–9, 124
problem solving 17
producer/industrial goods 76, **78**
product differentiation 76
production 4, 5–6, 150–4
  batch 150, 151–2, 153, **154**
  costs 104
  factors of 106
  mass 15
  methods of 151–3
  primary 4, **7**
  secondary 4, **7**
productivity 28
products 4, 5–6, 74–7
  augmented 75
  change 74–5, 77
  definition **78**
  improved 16, 17, 77
  life cycle 71, 76, **78**
  and markets 11
  mix 75, **78**
  new 16–17
  and place 86
  and promotion 80
  pull strategies 86
  push strategies 86
  range 75, **78**
  selling 42
  substitutes 69, **72**
  see also goods; services
professional indemnity insurance 145
profit 3–4, 5, 110–15
  and business location 58
  calculation 104, 111–12, 113
  and customer service 166

definition **109**, 113
  gross 112, **115**
  maximisation 28, 112, **115**
  net 112, **115**
  retained 93, **97**
  and revenue 105
  as target 28, 29
profit and loss account 111–12
promotion 69, 70, 71, 76, 79–84, **84**
  above-the-line expenditure 80
  advertising 79–80, 82–3, **84**
  below-the-line expenditure 80
  efficacy 82
  prices 70, 80
promotion (staff) 134
Prontaprint 21
psychological point pricing 69
public limited companies 51, 52, 108
public relations 80, 83, **84**
publicity 40, **44**
Pugh, Graham 55
Pugh, Ian 55
pull strategies 86
push strategies 86

qualitative data 66
quality
  of goods 170
  of service 167
quantitative data 66
quaternary sector 156
questionnaires 65, **67**, 168
quotes 144, **148**

rates 36
raw materials 4, 15, **19**, 158
re-mortgaging 95
recession 147, **148**
recognition 134
record keeping 162
recruiting staff 124–8, **128**
  external recruitment 126
  internal recruitment 126
Reed, Richard 50
Reggae Reggae Sauce 79–80
research and development 100
resources 28, 106
restaurants 26–7, 71
retail 56, 157

revenue 4, 15, 46, 104–7
  advertising 104
  and break-even 111
  and cash flow 118, 119, 120
  definition **19**, **49**, **109**
  and profit 110, 111–12, 113
  spreading 118, 119
  total 113
  see also turnover
rewards 15
  monetary 135, 136
  non-monetary 135
Richer Sounds 134–5
risk
  and liability status 46
  management 17
  minimisation 47–8
  taking 14–19
risk capital 17
road systems 56, 58
Roots, Levi 79–80
royalties 21, 22, **25**
Ryanair 68

salaries 129, 131, 134
Sale of Goods Act 170
sale-or-return basis 96
satellite navigation systems 162
satisfaction 28
  customer 29, 166–7, **168**
  job 132
secondary industries 158
  see also manufacturing
security 94, 95, **97**
selection 127, **128**
selling 42
services 4, 5–6, 76
  defence 157
  definition 156
  education 157
  financial 157
  health 157
  improved 17
  leisure 157
  new 16–17
  provision 155–9
  retailing 157
shareholders 35, 51, **54**
shares 35, 52, 131
short listing 127

Index

Silverjet 68
skill specialisation 3
   see also deskilling
skilled labour 151
small businesses
   and ICT 160–4
   and promotion 81–2
small claims court 144, 145–7
Small Firm Loan Guarantee scheme 100
smart cards 160, **164**
SMART targets 28, 29
Smith, Daniel 165
social enterprises 5
social responsibility 28, 30, **32**, 134
sole traders 110
speculation 43
sponsorships 80, 82, 83
SportStars 155, 156
staff recruitment 124–8
staff rewards 129–33
   monetary 130, 132
   non-monetary 130, 132
stakeholders 34–9, **39**
   creditors 36, **39**
   customers 35–6, 37
   definition 35
   employees 35, 37
   environment 37–8
   external 36
   internal 36
   local communities 36, 37–8, **39**
   shareholders 35
   suppliers 36
starting a business 33–60
   business location 55–60
   business structure 45–9, 50–4
   franchises 23–4
   limited liability companies 48, 50–4
   planning an enterprise 40–4
   stakeholders 34–9
   start-up (sunk) costs 41, 43
   unlimited liability 46–8

stationery 81
statistics 81
stock 112
Streetcar 160–2
Style Gardens 55, 56
subsistence level 3
substitutes 69, **72**
Subway 20, 23
suggestion schemes 134, **138**
suing 53
SuperJam 14
suppliers 36, 144, **148**
supply 9, **13**, 63
surplus 120, **122**
surveys 65, 167
sustainability 30

target markets 87, **90**
targets 27–9, 111
tax authorities 108
tax relief 100, **103**
tax returns 145
taxes 145
Taylor, James 155, 156
Taylor Wimpey 92
teachers, supply 124
teamwork 17, 136
technology 12
   integration 74
   and market trends 74
   and products 74, 75
   see also ICT
tertiary industries 4, **7**, 158
   see also services
Tesco 16
Tours4.com 165–7
toys 171
trade 3
Trade Descriptions Act 170
Trade Marks [TM] 169
Trading Standards 169, 172, **173**
transport 86
trial periods 127
turnover 21, **25**, 155, **159**
   see also revenue

UK Intellectual Property Office (UKIPO) 99
UK Trade and Investment 99
unemployment 35, **39**, 102
unique selling points (USPs) 42, 58, **60**
Universal 85
unlimited liability 46–8
utilities 118, **122**

V2Go 62, 63, 64
Valentin, Andre 160
value
   adding 75
   for money 69, **72**
VAT (value added tax) 145
Vegetarian Society 62, 63
venture capital/capitalists 17, 94
videos 74, 75
Vika, Paula 45, 47
viral advertising 83
Virgin 16, 24, 51, 130
volunteer work 135

wages 106, 125, 129–31, 135–6
   basic 129, **133**
   national minimum 131, 139, **143**
   performance-related pay 132
wants 5
warranties 66
websites 89
'what if' predictions 111–12
wheat 8
Whittaker, James 62
women, working 4
word processing 162
'word-of-mouth' 80, 81, 166
working hours
   contracted 130, **133**
   flexible 142
Wright, Jon 50
write offs 147, **148**

young entrepreneurs 14, 15, 40